PORTUGAL

ROY CAMPBELL

PORTUGAL

HENRY REGNERY COMPANY
Chicago 1958

©

ROY CAMPBELL
SOUTH AFRICAN
1957

Set in Fournier and printed in Great Britain by
RICHARD CLAY AND COMPANY, LTD
BUNGAY, SUFFOLK

Contents

Illustrations

Introduction

PORTUGAL occupies a little more than a fifth of the Iberian peninsula. With a coastline measuring 530 miles, and a Spanish frontier on the north and east measuring 784 miles, it covers an area of about 35,000 square miles. In Europe, apart from Portugal itself, the Azores, Madeira, and the Savage Islands, between Madeira and the Canaries, all belong to the Portuguese. In Africa the Portuguese own the islands of Cape Verde, Santo Fome and Principe, and (on the mainland) Portuguese Guinea, and the vast territories of Angola and Moçambique. In Asia, the Indian colonies of Goa, Diu, and Damão, with the Chinese colony of Macau and the Polynesian island of Timor, complete the total of 1,360,000 square miles ruled by the Portuguese throughout the world, with a population of 20,000,000, of whom 8,500,000 reside in the Mother country.

Portuguese culture, language, and influence, however, extend far outside the boundaries of the present empire. In the United States there is a very large Portuguese community which preserves its native language and customs. Together with the vast Portuguese-speaking population of Brazil, the number of people using the Portuguese language in the world today totals well above 70,000,000.

Portugal is bound very closely culturally, economically, and in natural affection to Brazil. In Portugal itself, the majority of the population is rural. The two largest cities, Lisbon and Oporto, have roughly 800,000 and 300,000 inhabitants respectively. Less than a quarter of the population lives in towns of over 10,000 inhabitants. The predominance of the rural population ensures the conservation of human, racial, traditional, and hereditary values, morals, and customs, so that Portugal remains a national and human oasis, together with its neighbour Spain: in a Europe whose nations are rapidly becoming dehumanized, denationalized, and stereotyped as machine-fodder under the persuasion of American commercial capitalism and the coercion of Soviet state-capitalism, both of which subordinate the human soul and body to abstract, academic considerations of economics, technology, and science.

In this book I write about the only country in Europe which, because of two miracles, the honesty, valour, and genius of a statesman of peasant stock, Salazar, and the perfectly provable appearance of the Mother of God, the snake-treader, Eve, at Fatima, is on the upward grade. The freemasons used torture on tiny children to try to disprove the latter miracle, but the children wore them out even though threatened with being boiled in oil! I put Salazar first because it is a greater miracle that a statesman should be clean, than that Our Lady should be kind. Thirty years ago Portugal was the most bankrupt, scruffy, and disreputable country in Europe, because of the forcible impositions on her of masonic governments. Today she is the only country in Europe (bar one) which has not lost prestige, but gained it.

This remarkable rebirth has taken place under the inspired guidance of Salazar, who has reformed his country out of chaos in a manner worthy of the original father of Portugal, Dom Afonso Henriques, under whom the country emerged as a separate nation in the twelfth century.

Before Salazar, Portugal had undergone an almost continuous decline from the great days of the Golden Age, when a land of only a million souls gave birth to *conquistadores* who set forth with radiant valour to found one of the greatest maritime empires the world has ever known. Most remarkably, it has survived almost intact, at least spiritually, and is still one of the largest, and perhaps the greatest, empire in the world today. More than that, it has shared in the rebirth which has saved the mother country. This is not only a living testimony to the wisdom of Dr. Salazar, but also to the incredible vitality of those early Portuguese who built up so much that was enduring with so few people and with such slender resources.

Portugal and the Portuguese overseas possessions are governed and live so quietly that they are seldom in the news. In the African possessions there is no 'native question' because the Portuguese, a fundamentally Christian and charitable people, have no time for any kind of racial discrimination which is not strictly necessary and practical. One such possession, Goa, has however been in the news—but only to prove the point. People are apt to forget that when Goa was a flourishing colony, 'India' did not exist. Now, the Goanese are first and foremost Portuguese, and have not the least desire to break with a country to whom they owe their existence, their opportunities, and a large part of their unique civilization.

Portuguese civilization and culture bear witness to Portugal's great and special gift to the world: an intense, heroic, and enduring humanity. It is this survival of the human element, quite as much as any attractions of climate, scenery, and architecture, that brings so many foreign residents and tourists to Portugal. That is my excuse for adding to the many books written in English about Portugal recently: I am indebted to the authors of *They Went to Portugal*, *The Selective Traveller in Portugal*, *Portugal and Madeira*, *Blue Moon in Portugal*, and other excellent books for guidance in avoiding subjects that they have treated so much better already than I could have done. I have not tried to write a travel-book, or a guide-book, or a text-book about Portugal. This is a personal book, about a country which I love and admire and about a people among whom I can number countless friends in all walks of life. I have one advantage over most previous writers—I have worked with my hands. Portugal is a marine country, and I have been a sailor and fisherman; it is an agricultural country, and I have grown my own wine, wheat, and oil; it is a country of livestock and of horses and horsemen, and I have been cattleman, horse-trader, and picador. It is an intensely poetic country, and it is the country of *saudade*, that mysterious melancholy which sighs at the back of every joy, delight, and pleasure like the wind in the pines.

This is a book about my personal contacts with a land of lovely contrasts and delightful people, from the figs and almonds of the Algarve, in the deep South, to the green Elysium of woods and streams which is the Minho, from the uplands of Tras-os-Montes, harsh as the cry of a wild bird, to the corn-swept prairies of the Alentejo, from the clanging, song-haunted streets of Lisbon to the wolf-bare silences of the Mountains of the Star.

It is a book about people I have met and things I have seen and done in the country which is now my home.

R. C.

CHAPTER ONE

Romans and Celts

THE ROMANS divided the Iberian peninsula into three Provinces. The Tarraconensis (by far the largest) extended finally from the Pyrenees to Finisterre, cutting off from Lusitania the part of Portugal included between the Douro and the Minho, and the rest of Galicia. The Baetica Province was more or less what is today the modern Andalusia, the smallest in area, if not in importance, of the three divisions. Lusitania was roughly what Portugal is today, but, apart from the amputation of the land north of the Douro, it differed in containing a considerable part of central, western Spain extending to Talavera de la Reina (Augustobriga) and Toledo, and enclosing the whole of the Sierra de Gredos, with Salamanca in the north, and Badajoz and Merida in the south. Being farthest from Rome, and the last of the provinces to be conquered, it was also the poorest in development until Augustus adopted it as his pet colony, and lavished such munificence on Emerita, or Merida, as to make her and her surroundings the richest in Roman remains of all Iberia. Modern Portugal has grown richer along her coastline than in the interior because of her trade with her overseas empire; but Roman Portugal grew poorer in monuments, bridges, and aquaducts as it receded towards the sea from the frontiers of the rich Baetica, since there was more commerce with the Roman metropolis by land than by sea. The result is that the most interesting part of Portugal from the point of view of Roman archæology is in the south-west, where many finds are being made. In the long years of stagnation which preceded the present regime, less building, engineering, road-building, mining, and excavations was done in two centuries than in the last ten years, especially down in that part of the country which is now the most backward, though in Roman times it was the most progressive.

If few of these finds are of great size, many of them are of great interest and beauty, and can be seen in various local museums, such as that at Evora, that of Marchado in Coimbra, and the Ethnological Museum of Belem, on the way to Estoril from Lisbon. When I was on leave in 1938 during the Spanish War at Abicada, near Cape St. Vincent, I was present at the digging up of a fine Roman villa with mosaics and frescoes, which were taken to the museum at Lagos, where they can still be seen. Along the same coast, about fifteen and a half miles from the Spanish frontier, near Tavira, is the unexplored site of the Roman settlement of Balsa. The peasants here on the farms *de Antas* and *Torre de Ares* —significant names—are always unearthing fragments of tiles, masonry, statues, columns, and mosaics. This part of the country has a beautiful climate, conducive to the building of luxury villas by retired Roman magistrates and the like. Villas are rare in other parts of Portugal, where the Celtic way of building dwellings predominated until comparatively late in the Roman colonization. All the greatest monuments of the old Lusitania are to be found just over the Spanish border.

Some people consider the Alcantara bridge the finest Roman monument in the whole peninsula, next to that half-mile or so of uncemented stone aqueduct at Segovia, which is still in use, and seems a miracle of airy balance and skill. When I look at that towering, labyrinthine conjuring trick of loose stones, it makes me hold my breath as if I were watching an elephant dancing on a tight-rope of spider-thread hundreds of feet in the air: one feels that if a single stone were to give way, the whole of the miraculous fabric would crash down and wipe out the inhabitants. The bridge of Alcantara (which is just at the Spanish border near Vilar Formoso, on one of the main roads into Portugal from Madrid) gives one the very opposite sensation, one of such massive solidity that not even an earthquake could shift it. The Tagus has many fine bridges, from the Moorish Alcantara at Toledo to the Roman one at Talavera, down to the ultra-modern one at Vila Franca connecting Estremadura with the Alentejo: but the Roman Alcantara is the most impressive of the lot. The name Alcantara is to be found everywhere from the Suez Canal to Central Spain: it is the Arab word for 'bridge', ford, or ferry, and the name of one of the chief docks of Lisbon, whence the largest liners leave for America.

This Roman bridge of Alcantara is about ten yards wide, two hundred yards long, and fifty high. It spans a low, rugged canyon with six beautiful arches. In the middle, surmounting the whole bridge, is a high lateral arch over the roadway, which may have served as a toll-gate. It was built under the Emperor Trajan, himself an Iberian by birth and a native of what is perhaps the most picturesque village in all the peninsula, Pedraza, like an eyrie, in the ranges, with a colossal castle and a square surrounded with marble pillars, where they have an annual bullfight. There is another fine Roman bridge at Chaves in the very north of Portugal: it is low, but long, with about fifteen arches, and a massive cylindrical stone 'signpost' in the middle inscribed in Latin with the information that it connects Braga (Bracara Augusta) with Astorga.

In spite of being such very poor builders, the Celts and Celtiberians are responsible for some of the greatest architectural wonders of antiquity. Even the Great Wall of China owes its existence to nomadic shepherds and cattlemen mounted on small ponies who could scarcely even build mud huts: and great walls will always be found in the vicinity of Celtiberian communities, which, with the exception of the Jews, have always proved the most difficult race to dominate, assimilate, and domesticate by Romans and Teutons alike. In moral fibre and will-power the Jew compares to the average European as the latter does to an African native; his civilization, without decaying in any way, unlike the Egyptian or the Cretan, has given him a start by several thousand years. The Celtic race is similarly pertinacious owing to having had (if not a civilization) such a set, unchanging way of life, for so many thousands of years, as to confirm and ingrain its racial characteristics in such a way that, in any interbreeding

with other races, a Celt's faults, virtues, weaknesses, and vices are
sure to predominate over those of his mate, both in his offspring
and descendants. We have the case in Natal of polygamists, the
white 'Zulu' chieftains, Fynn, a western Irishman, and Dunn, a
lowland Scottish Anglo-Saxon, both of whom left thousands of
descendants. Even for his own sons Dunn had a big school with
house-masters and about ten acres of playing-fields. The tawny-
coloured great-grandsons of Dunn are today distinguishable only
by name: but even in North Africa, in the War, amongst the
great-great-great-great-grandsons of Fynn in the South African
Coloured Corps, I recognized three Fynns by their features and
called them by name: and they were quite used to it! They are
not in any way superior to the Dunns, only more easily recognizable through transmitted features.

Nowhere in the world has the struggle between the Celtiberian herdsmen and the Roman bread-eater recorded itself
more imposingly in stone or more dramatically in history than
in Lusitania, not even in Britain, where the same feud was responsible for Hadrian's and other great walls. That the Cale-
donians were exactly the same people who had migrated through
Ireland is proved not only by the sword-dance, certain reels,
dances, and tunes, but also by the similarity of the protective
walls, if we compare the great walls round Lugo with those
across the lowlands of Scotland, and the necessitation of an
identical type of warfare and fortification. But the chief link between Scotland and Portugal is in the fact that when they left
Iberia, the Celts brought their boars along with them. These
stone boars, whose statues are to be found all through northern
Spain and Portugal, especially at Murça and Braganza, were sym-
bols both of royalty and fertility, because, with the Celts, the two
were synonymous—the kings or chiefs being given the first
night with all brides in order to promulgate valour and prowess.
Fertility with the Celts, who breed slowly compared with quick-
breeding races like the Teutons, had an enhanced value.

The Celtiberian chief was nearly always the finest warrior, and
the bravest man of his tribe or clan, as in the case of Variathus in

Portugal, and, down to almost modern times, Lochiel in Scotland. This was not only a Celtic feature but a European one. Even kings were expected to be their own best soldiers: not only as in the case of King Dom Sebastian and King Dom Pedro 'the Cruel' (or 'the Just' as the people called him in Portugal), but of Richard Cœur de Lion, Ferdinand of Aragon, the Emperor Charles V, Robert Bruce, and other kings elsewhere. Even the weak-willed Edward II, of England, was reported to have fought better than all the Anglo-Normans at Bannockburn, and that was in the days when Englishmen and lowland Scotsmen were 'all Rolands and Olivers' according to Froissart. So it shows what was expected of a king. In this Froissart was referring chiefly to lowlanders, since the highlanders were mainly engaged in feuds with each other: it was only well on in the eighteenth century that they attempted to combine, but without much success. Though very brave men, they could never organize themselves. The same was true of their early Lusitanian ancestors. It was generally when the Celts acquired a foreign chief like Sertorious or Montrose that they could put up a determined organized resistance. Otherwise it was simply their reckless courage and ferocity that protected them for so long.

There are signs in the north of Portugal and Galicia that the Romans never fully conquered those parts, any more than they did the Highlands of Scotland, though they had a big lighthouse, still known today as the Tower of Hercules, at Finisterre, near La Coruña. The huge wall round Lugo is a sign that it was the Romans and not the Lusitanians who required the most defence. It is significant, too, that this Celtic part was never conquered by the Moors: but the Reconquest started from there. Even at Numantia, Scipio had to build a huge wall and a moat round the town before he could take it. After eating all their Roman prisoners, the Numantines made a great fire in the central square, on which they placed everything of value, then slew all their wives and children, and perished in the flames, so that not one inhabitant was left to grace the Roman triumph. Perhaps the most heart-rending play every written is Cervantes' *Siege of*

Numancia. This was by no means the only case of Celtiberian mass-suicide rather than surrender. Astapa and Saguntum similarly committed suicide to the last man, though the latter were well outside the Lusitanian area.

The big stone boar carved in the rock at Dunadd in Argyll-shire is the brother of that at Murça in northern Portugal, and those at Segovia, Guisando, Braganza, and other places. Like that of Murça, the Scottish one is accompanied by a hollow bowl to contain the oil of anointment. The very ancient clan whose name I bear landed in western Scotland in about the first century B.C. Not only did they carve a boar identical with those of northern Portugal in the solid rock twenty centuries ago, but they wear it to this day as their tribal crest or totem in their glengarries, and use a very similar dark green tartan to many of the shirts to be seen on the fishermen in Nazaré, in northern Portugal.

When Queen Victoria rebuked the Kaiser for objecting to her daughter, his cousin, marrying a Campbell 'dukeling', she cannot have been instructed in the swineology of the family into which she was marrying her daughter, for she wired to her nephew the Kaiser: 'The Campbells were the Lords of the Isles when the Hohenzollerns were still herding swine.' Little she knew of our long association with these animals, though I notice that people of my name never eat pork. We were of the poorer peasant stock, legitimately unrelated to our dukes, and, until my father's time, in spite of transposition abroad, stuck loyally and instinctively to the taboo. Whether it is from the very sound hygienic reasons for not eating pork which condition the Semitic, Muslim, and Jewish attitude to it, or because it is a totem-taboo on the badge of our clan, I never found out. I know that my ancestors, though objecting to eating wild boars or bush-pigs, or even tame pigs, never objected to killing them. On the contrary, like the French Government, they gave small awards to anyone who killed one on our estate in South Africa. Of all land animals, they are the most costly for their size and number in the damage they do. In fact the Government award (wherever they abound) for a wild pig is equal to that for that deadly enemy of the fishing industry, the porpoise. Only elephants or hippos do more damage, but sporadically, not systematically, to gardens. Wild pigs are even more destructive to potatoes, beets, swedes, groundnuts, and roots in general, as they work chiefly underground. Of all the wild animals on the Iberian peninsula they are the fiercest, including bears and wolves. Although wolves can become really nasty in the winter, they are usually retiring.

To deal with a big wild boar requires a whole pack of dogs, and even then you are quite likely to lose half a dozen. They are very tenacious of life, extremely cunning, wizards in camouflage, and both in Europe and Africa outlast nearly all other wild animals in remaining undetected in urbanized areas. Though for cunning foxes and wolves are hard to beat, yet for their enormous size, wild boars are even greater dissimulators, and they are particularly fond of the dwarf oak scrub and its acorns, which abound in Portugal and Spain. One of the keepers of the park at Kenwood, well inside London, killed ten wild foxes in a year, and I put him on the air at the B.B.C. to tell London all about its wild life; and last time I was in Toronto a large 'stray dog' doing the rounds of the dustbins proved, on police investigation, to be a full-grown timber-wolf. But these wild canine incursions partake of the nature of nocturnal raids. Wild boars actually live day and night unseen, except for their tracks, within full view of big Portuguese cities, at the very doors of civilization, for years, just as the Celtiberians lived at the very gates of the Roman civilization without being tamed or conquered. I had a surprising proof, well within sight of the suburbs of Marseilles and its airport of Marignine, of the ability of wild boars to survive in civilization. But for a fire in the pinewoods they would still be there. But they were forced (a huge boar and two sows) by the heat to swim out on to the lake of Berre, where, in the dark, they caught their feet in our sardine-nets and were drowned while we slept in the boat beside them. Imagine our surprise at the strange catch in our nets next morning! In Portugal they abound most on the Guadiana, in sight of their earthly Paradise across the river, the Sierra Morena, where there are more to the acre than the square mile

B

elsewhere in Europe. There are also many in the Serra da Estrela.

Viriathus, whose tactics were those of the wounded wild boar, which are always to work round so as to be able to get a downward charge of the greatest momentum and impetus, would as naturally choose a wild boar for his tribal totem as his Caledonian descendants, whose fighting tactics were the same, should carry that totem with them to Scotland. The Lusitanians under both Sertorius and Viriathus carried their Roman wars far out of Lusitanian territory.

Celtiberian villages consisted of round houses with stone walls to the height of about a yard, which can still be seen, though the adobe superstructure with which the building was completed has entirely disappeared. The Celtiberians were physically superior to the Romans, which is saying a great deal, when you remember the two world's-record infantry marches of Claudius Nero, testified to by Carthaginians and Romans alike. In one of these marches his army did fifty-five miles a day for six days, fighting and winning a stiff pitched battle on the third day. This beats anything in ancient or modern history, even when Sir John Moore was retreating for all he was worth with the Highland Light Infantry to win the famous technical victory at La Coruña, which inspired one of the very few good military poems in English (apart from Drayton's *Agincourt*, Bloomfield's *Old Soldier*, Campbell's *Hohenlinden* and *Soldier's Dream*, and Dryden's *Annus Mirabilis*), which, for want of anything bigger (it could hardly be better), stands to England as the *Lusiads* stand to Portugal. The proof that the Celtiberian was physically superior to the Roman is easily seen in the fact that the Celtic tactics (finally outmoded and outnumbered at Culloden Moor) were to *seek* the enemy, and the Roman tactics were to evade the enemy behind walls and to fight with missiles. The Celtic towns were built on eminences, but not fortified, because it is more pleasurable and effective to charge downhill than uphill. The Celtiberian's rampart was his personal prowess and courage. What kept the enemy at the most respectful distance was to try to get at him. The Romans could only make headway against them either by fortification or bribing fellow-Celtiberians to attack them. Viriathus won all his battles. The speeches of the Roman Wellington, Scipio, are an open admission of Roman inferiority as soldiers. His tactics against the Lusitanians at Numantia are an even greater admission. In the twelve-year siege of 8,000 Numantines (with only 2,000 fighting men) by an army varying from 60,000 to 80,000 Romans (the victors of Hannibal) the Numantines supported themselves by raiding and looting the Roman camp in exactly the same way as the Portuguese and Spanish guerilla fighters got their arms, ammunition, and supplies from the French in the Napoleonic wars and from the Internationals in the Civil War. Both the sieges of the Hermitage and the Alcazar would have come roughly within the technical boundaries of Roman Lusitania, and the methods were exactly the same as those used in Numantia. Captain Cortes and a handful of some sixty Civil Guards lived for ten months in the unfortified Hermitage of Santa Murea de la Cabeza on the food and ammunition which they took chiefly from the 16th French International Tank Brigade, among other troops besieging them, till they were finally wiped out, with scarcely any survivors, except the wounded, and those were butchered.

Similar sorties to loot and raid also happened at the Alcazar when the Russian bosses Ilya Ehrenburg and Rosenburg imagined that every inhabitant of Toledo had been terrorized into subjection by such pleasant resources as loosing all criminals, inciting them 'to do their stuff' and commit fearsome babooneries, including those from the lunatic asylum, which, in Toledo, is the Broadmoor of Spain, when suddenly the 'doomed garrison' sailed out and grabbed a million rounds of ammunition from the arms factory by the Tagus and some hundreds of sacks of wheat from the mill. The whole town was twice evacuated of inhabitants when two mines, one of two tons of dynamite and one of seven tons, were let off under the building; in both cases 5,000 shock troops, mostly French, stormed the building immediately after the explosion, and on the second occasion the red flag with hammer and sickle was flying from the north-eastern tower. In each case the garrison, though half-stunned, made such spirited sorties that the Internationals fled. When Captain Alba was killed after escaping through the sewers, I had to get out with the news that the garrison was still holding out, which I did on 2 August 1936,[1] so I missed both the sorties; but saw them later on the films captured from the Reds, who had reported the surrender of the garrison more times than Goebbels did the sinking of the *Ark Royal*, so it became absolutely necessary to get the truth out to the Nationalists. As in the Luso-Spanish sieges of Numantia, Estepa, and Saguntum, it was the besiegers who entrenched themselves at the Hermitage and the Alcazar. But if you look at the *Illustrated London News* or *L'Illustration* of those times, you will see the Internationals all crouching beside barricades and trenches cut in the main street leading up to the Plaza de Zodocover. 9,600 shells were fired into the Alcazar, quite apart from aerial bombardments, yet it lasted three months.

Cervantes, in his play of *Numancia*, follows Livy about as closely as Shakespeare follows Plutarch in *Coriolanus*, *Antony and Cleopatra*, and *Julius Cæsar*: that is to say he verifies the main speeches and harangues of the two Scipio brothers, and makes up one for Marius, who was then only a sergeant-major, though the smartness of his equipment and his keenness as a soldier had already signalized him to his Commander-in-Chief. Cervantes' verse, at its best, does not rise to the same heights as Shakespeare's, but as Shelley says, if it is not pure poetry it is about as good a substitute for it as could be possibly imagined. The play itself is a gigantic work of genius chiefly because of the characterization. Cervantes is said 'to have laughed away the chivalry of Spain' in *Don Quixote*. I think that if readers of *Don Quixote* were to start by reading that wonderful hymn to Celtiberian valour and chivalry which is the *Numancia*, they would draw another meaning from *Don Quixote*, and see that the author is passionately on the side of the Knight of the Sad Countenance,

[1] See *Daily Express* 6 August 1936: full page badly misreported interview entitled 'British Bullfighter escapes from the flames. Garrison still holds out.'

and that he is holding the matter-of-fact world up to scorn for falling short of the noble dreams of the Knight.

The great Lusitanian hero Viriathus had to be got rid of by bribing other Celtiberians to murder him. This is the weakness of all Celts: they seem to enjoy fighting each other more than their common enemy, and the descendants of Viriathus in the north of Scotland wasted centuries in petty clan feuds which, even at critical moments like Killikrankie and Culloden, always took precedence over their quarrel with the common enemy. It was only when disciplined first by the Romans and then by the English that the Celtiberians reached their perfection as soldiers both under Cæsar's cavalry general Labinus and at a much later period, under Wellington's cavalry general, Sir Benjamin Durban (the godfather of my home town), when the Portuguese cavalry acted as the spearhead of the British advance up the Tagus and the Portuguese infantry fought shoulder to shoulder with their Highland cousins in 'the thin red line' at Albuera, and at the storming of Badajoz, both just over the border, and once a part of Portugal. Queen Victoria did not live to see it, but the old boars of Murça and Dunadd lived to repay her patronage in marrying her daughter to one of their chiefs, for it is the wearers of the boar's-head crest carried from Braganza and Murça to Argyllshire, who have collected many of the coveted trophies to which the Great Queen gave her name, the Victoria Cross, of which in the last few wars the Campbells have won more than any other two names combined.

Before civilization can be perfected, the wheat-eating, organized, agricultural, and urbanized culture must always conquer and absorb that of the herdsmen, shepherds, and swine-herds. It is the old story of Cain and Abel, and it embodies the whole history of the human race.

The hunter developed into a herdsman centuries before the first agricultural village took shape in about 6700 B.C. at Jarmo in Mesopotamia. Hunting and herdsmanship are schools of courage and cunning: they teach self-reliance, individualism, independence, which are at once the strength and weakness of the Celt, and the reason for his inability to organize, build, or collectivize. Everywhere in human history throughout the world fortune has decided in favour of the stationary, sedentary, plodding plough-man. Cain, against the roving herdsman, Abel, his less progressive brother.

From the agriculturalists, industrial, and materialistic peoples we derive laws, machines, cities, fortifications, roads, and industries. The herdsmen had the leisure to dream, and to them civilization owes its poetry, philosophy, astronomy, music, and mathematics. Abel is the lover of God, whom the practical Cain killed for driving his goat too near the furrow. . . . There you have the whole drama of human progress throughout the world.

It would appear that whereas Cain adapts his environment to his body by building roofs and walls around it, filling mattresses with feathers, centrally heating his houses, and seating himself at meals or reclining in the Roman fashion, Abel avoids discomfort by hardening his body, and adapting it to his environment instead of vice versa. Some of the shepherds to this day sleep standing up or leaning against a rock or a tree. They are often clothed in skins of which the coats are known as *pellicos* and the pants as *safões*. They are generally unarmed except for slings and cudgels. Their toughness is proved several times every year against wolves, which abound in the Serra da Estrela. The year before last, a small boy of fourteen, having the appropriate surname of Pãoduro, or Hardbread, killed a wolf two metres long with a stone, when it attacked his sheep; and I have seen a hefty peasant girl attack and kill one with a cudgel, when she cornered it during a 'drive'.

It is round Coimbra that the Roman remains have been most exhaustively explored and brought to light: but Evora has a beautiful ruin of a temple of Diana. Sertorius was her great devotee, and he founded the city as his first capital or centre of resistance, before he made himself master of the whole peninsula and shifted his capital right up to the edge of the Pyrenees at Huesca. There was something highly poetical about this extraordinary man which endeared him irresistibly to the Celts, though there was a certain amount of trickery in his pretence to be Diana's favoured Endymion. He caught an albino fawn one day while hunting, made a pet of it, adorned it with gold earrings and a necklace, and taught it to nuzzle into his ear as if it were whispering to him. By this means, whenever he had good news of victory brought secretly to him, he pretended the doe had brought him the news from Diana. He organized first the Lusitanians and then the whole of the Celtiberian tribes into an invincible army with which he triumphed time and again over Pompey, Metullus, and other famous commanders who were sent against him. Although he was a highborn Roman he had many affinities with the Celts, and at the very beginning of his career, when serving under Marius, distinguished himself by entering their lines disguised as one of them, and apparently speaking their language. Like Viriathus, he was eventually got rid of by treacherous assassination, but it is good to know that the traitors for once all got exactly what they deserved, even more so than in the case of Julius Cæsar. Perpeura, the ringleader of the assassins, on supplanting Sertorius, was easily overthrown by Pompey; and thinking to beg his life from the latter, offered to show him a mass of letters convicting many principal Romans of conspiracy with Sertorius. Pompey nobly burned all these letters without looking at them. 'Of the rest of the conspirators,' concludes Plutarch, 'some were taken and slain by the command of Pompey, others fled to Africa and were set upon by Moors and run through with their darts; and in a short time only Aufidius was left alive, hiding in an obscure village in Spain, where he died, an old man, in extreme poverty, detested by all.'

CHAPTER TWO

Elysian Fields

PORTUGAL DOES a vast trade in fresh fruit. In fact after cork, wine, canned fish, and olive oil, her export trade in oranges, lemons, melons, pineapples, dried figs, and almonds comes fifth. Of these fruit trades the orange trade is by far the most important.

Oranges were supposed to be the original golden apples of the Hesperides which Hercules, in one of his 'labours', was sent in search of to the Western Land of the evening star which is obviously Portugal. The westernmost point of the Continent of Europe is the Cabo da Roca, where I live. We live in a time when tradition and myth are being asserted and confirmed more and more by archæological investigation. This process of the justification of myth and poetry by science has been going on ever since Schliemann and Evans confirmed the siege of Troy and the myths of Crete, at the end of the last century, to the discomfiture of all those scientific pedants who tried to dismiss them as 'allegories'. Almost the whole of English philosophy and thought during the last century can be said to have been founded on the Piltdown skull, which, as early as 1932, in the *Revista Zoologica* of Barcelona, I denounced as a fraud, merely from seeing a photograph of it. Now even the anatomists have admitted the fraud, and this shameful and humiliating fake, for which a great nation repudiated the inspiring truths of the Old Testament, has been 'knocked on the head' for the sixer it deserves, while investigators like Sir Charles Marston have unearthed incontrovertible evidence for the truth of the Flood, the Walls of Jericho, the destruction of Sodom and Gomorrah, and all the wonders of God, which were dismissed for the most glaringly obvious osseous fake that was ever set eyes on by a lot of superstitious blockheads.

24

Therefore, while admitting what the 'scientists' tell us—that a certain subspecies of sweet orange was introduced to Europe from China, the *citrus aurantium sinensis*—I adhere to the ancient *tradition* that oranges are indigenous to this Peninsula and that they were the 'apples of the daughters of the Evening Star', especially the wild orange, which English people use for making marmalade, and which we call the Seville orange, *citrus aurantium amarum*. I would also claim as indigenous the noble variety of sweet orange that reaches its full aureate splendour, rotundity, lusciousness, and sweetness in the district of Vidigueira, that oasis in the semi-desert Alentejo. I have seen only one district in the world that can rival it, and that is the coast around Valencia and Alicante, which surpasses Vidigueira in the quantity of oranges it produces per hectare, but falls far short of it in the quality; although those small Valencian blood-oranges have one striking advantage, in that they never go bad in their own climate, but can be kept for months, while the juice dissolves the pulp within them; then they shrink to small, tough, leathery bags, containing nothing but juice, in which state the peasants work them with their hands till they are soft. Making a hole in the rind, one can then *literally drink* the whole orange except for its thin, leathery shell. In that way they are delicious, but when fresh they cannot hold a candle to the fresh super-orange of Vidigueira, the Garden of the Hesperides.

With the Serra of Mendo for its background, pouring with rills, it revels in the thickest and greenest vegetation and the deepest of purple shades to be found south of the Tagus, where it nurses what is perhaps the most privileged and wealthy working population in Portugal, except that of the village and ranch of Mugem, under the tutelage of its all-providing fairy godmother, the Marquesa de Cadaval, who gives every one of her workers a bit of land of his own. On this rich soil of Vidigueira, to the creak and hum of a hundred busy water-wheels, vineyards alternate with apple orchards and orange groves for miles. There are 142 properties, bursting with green, vigorous sap. Here all the Moorish arts of irrigation (even by switching runnels with one's bare toe from one field to another!); of making hotbeds and nurseries; of pruning; of grafting oranges to lemons, and either to apples; and of cutting 'forks'—are to be seen in all their pristine glory. That Arab blood still runs in the veins of some of the Alentejo peasants is evident from the way they cherish water and trees, even where they are most plentiful. Only a race of people born and bred on the Sahara, and originating from the Arabian deserts, could handle water with such delicacy, love, and tenderness, or treat green trees as if they were some sort of benevolent divinity. I have seen peasants exchange water-jars as we would wines of different vintages—'just for a taste'. They can recognize the various local fountains, sources, and streams for miles around by whether they taste of quartz, granite, watercress, moss, or gravel. I once gave a thirsty hunter at Linhó a sip from the water-jug which I had filled from my new well on my place on the top of the serra five miles away. He said, 'It's strange. I do not recognize this well, but from the taste of *saibrão* (gravelly soil) it must be from near the quarries at Chão d'Arcos.' It is from these very stones I am blasting from this quarry, now my property, that I am building my house on the spot, and the well is only thirty yards away! He knew nothing of a well having been sunk there. It is only that during the rains water flows above ground in a little freshet from which hunters drink. Yet he remembered the *taste* of the water. It is very common in Portugal, when there is running water beside a dusty road, to enshrine a fountain in pretty, blue, glazed tiles, with the inscription of some of the fluvial verses of Camões or Bernadim Ribeiro which it makes you feel fresh and cool to read even before you drink.

The shade of the orange-tree, even if we include the fragrant ozone-breathing shade of the big umbrella-pines, is the most delicious, and the most restful to lie in, since the green-black leaves make a very dark purple-black shadow that twinkles above one, even in the fiercest glare of a summer noon, like a frosty autumn night rustling with a million stars. The shade of an orange-tree is always fragrant, but when the *azahar*, or orange blossom, is on the winds, and the very mountains seem to be breathing it with rapture into their valley-deep lungs, it is as if the word shade took on its secondary ghostly meaning. The shadows of the orange-trees become the blessed shades of Elysium, as they dance on the slender tops of the asphodels (which flower with white stars, at the same time) without bending them. Later on, then, in winter, what a delight it is to lean one's gun and throw one's partridges and hares at the foot of an orange-tree, then reach into the starry twilight of the leaves for a globe of solid red gold, which, if you close your eyes when you taste it, makes you think of orange sunsets in green skies over the Kalahari, of beautiful women with red-gold hair and green eyes, of the Golden Fleece in Valerius Flaccus's *Argonauts*:

> Nubibus accensis similem aut cum veste recincta
> Labitur ardenti Thaumantias obvia Phoebo.

and above all of that wonderful symphony in orange and gold which Quevedo wrote on Lisi's orange-coloured hair:

> When you shake free your hair from all controlling
> Such thirst of beauty quickens my desire
> Over its surge, in red tornadoes rolling,
> My heart goes surfing on the waves of fire.
> Leander, who for love the tempest dares
> It lets a sea of flames its life consume,
> Icarus, at a sun whose rays are hairs
> Ignites its wings and glories in its doom.
> Charring its hopes, whose deaths I mourn, it strives
> Out of their ash to fan new phœnix lives
> That, dying of delight, new hopes embolden.
> Miser, yet poor, the golden doom I measure
> Of Midas, starved and mocked with stacks of treasure,
> Or Tantalus with streams that ran as golden.

One thinks also of Keats's wonderful lines:

> And here are 'apples' plucked from Syrian trees
> *In starlight* by the four Hesperides.

For whether one picks one of these Hesperidian apples by day or by night, it is always in that sparkle of starlight which animates the breathing shade of an orange-tree.

There is a small kind of orange, sweeter than any other I ever tasted, which seems to be indigenous only to Portugal. It has a very soft rind and flourishes chiefly in the country round Setúbal. The sour, wild orange is much superior to the domestic one in its medicinal qualities. The fruit is rich in the following vitamins (if my reader believes in such quaint old twentieth-century superstitions): A, B_1, B_2, C, and D. Infusions of orange-peel are taken as a tonic throughout southern France, Spain, and Portugal, though orange-peel is generally thrown away in England: but the 'Hyde Park Lancers', when

> Like grim knights-errant on their journey
> Couching their broomsticks tipped with pins
> I've watched them joust their dismal tourney
> Tent-pegging garbage into tins,

have often two smaller tins under their coats, which they use for cigarette ends and orange-peel, though they keep glowering around suspiciously to see if anyone is looking when they slip the orange-peel away. If you are curious about the life-story of the exported Portuguese orange keep your eyes on the H.P.L. If you watch them they leave the orange-peel and pretend to be more intent on shovelling papers and half-chewed buns into the big tins. But if you look away, they come back for the orange-peel, about which they behave in a furtive, self conscious manner, from which I take it they get a rake-off over and above their L.C.C. salaries from the jam factories or chemical manufacturers of bromides.

I first became interested in this London orange-peel industry because I am not only the ex-champion tent-pegger of the 5th Requété Cavalry Regiment and the old Imperial Light Horse, but I was once mistaken for a Hyde Park Lancer myself, by a short-sighted old gentleman, who led me to a mass of garbage, apparently the relics of a picnic, and said it was disgraceful. This was when Hyde Park Lancers wore great slouch hats, but without plumes or chin-straps. I was in the bush-hat of the King's African Rifles with a chin-strap and a great black plume of widow-bird's feathers, which the old man apparently did not notice, but I was clothed in army hospital-blues (somewhat like a scavenger's uniform) and was teaching my wounded hip to walk, painfully, with a stick—from which the half-blind old gentleman got the idea that I was a sanitary man prodding, not for my balance, but for garbage, and thereupon led me to a spot where my tent-pegging talents could be better employed. Since then I have always felt an *esprit de corps* with the H.P.L. Brigade, and I dare say I shall end up in them one day.

It was through this episode that I got an insight into the life-story of a Portuguese orange, which I always thought ended, after exportation, in an Englishman's stomach, but apparently that is more like the beginning than the end of its mysterious and slightly sinister Odyssey after it gets to England. The peel sheds the orange inside the Englishman, then comes back to rejoin its core after a trip round the jam factories weeks later.

An infusion of the leaves or the flowers of either the sour or the sweet orange (the sour is better) is a sedative, diaphoretic, antispasmodic tonic and febrifuge, efficacious in the case of indigestion, vomiting, palpitations, nervous coughs, hiccoughs, hysteria, etc. But it should never be taken if there is the slightest inflammation of the stomach.

The wood is being used now, as far superior to the yew of the old long-bow, for making bows to hunt big game, which is coming into fashion. It can drive an arrow clean through the heart of an elephant, and, as I recently proved on the Komati river in Moçambique, in front of journalists of two countries, will pierce a crocodile if shot on the 'Plimsoll-line' between back and belly, from the side (and I've even known a bullet jump, if placed an inch wrong in a side shot at a crocodile). It was one of the silliest things that ever happened, that after the handling of the carbine became a one-handed affair, the bow and arrow did not come back as an infantry weapon. For night-fighting it is soundless. There were only three in use (cut from sour orange-trees near Evora) at

the Battles of the Jarama, Brunete, and San Mateo, and we had to
get permission of Spanish high-up officers to use them—but you
ought to see the prisoners that turn up next day after some of
those silent arrows have gone about by night! Silent warfare of
this kind, with results, will clear whole trenches when rifle-fire
merely makes the enemy keep their heads down. What made the
Communist International Brigade of English Reds surrender at
San Mateo (apart from the Spanish Reds machine-gunning them
from the rear every time they tried to run away, which was
pretty often!) was getting into their trenches at night with double
thick, short orange-wood bows,[1] speaking English, pretending to
be homosexual (most Englishmen fall for that) and letting them
have it at point-blank range with barbless and featherless arrows,
short enough to bury themselves entirely. They did not know
(some of them do not know to this day, though I told my relative,
George Orwell) what was happening either to themselves or their
friends who were falling dead or wounded in the dark without
any sound of fire. When I told Orwell, whom I had previously
wounded, he recognized the cause of the panic. They were
scared to surrender to the Spaniards, but asked to surrender to the
Italian blackshirts, a unit more sissified (if that were possible) than
their own! So we had to send to the rear for Prince William Ros-
pigliosi (now *orange-farming* himself in Southern Rhodesia), and
he took the surrender which was partly due to two Portuguese
orange-wood bows of double thickness and third-shortness,
worked quietly at night by Legionary Sergeant Jerry Mannin,
transferred from O'Duffy's, and myself. It was my idea. The
only snag was that he nearly let fly at me in the pitch dark! These
bows were cut at Evora and they were strung with horse-tails
from Santarem. They did good work.

It is a sad truth that oranges in Portugal are generally labelled
from the big buying centres, rather than from the place where
they are grown, so a Vidigueira orange may arrive in England

---

[1] These took almost three times the pressure of an ordinary hunting bow.
Only Sgt. Mannin of the Legion, weighing 220 pounds, and myself, weighing
236, could stretch these bows to the required pressure.

with Portel, Evora, or Beja on the label, instead of Vidigueira. It
is only by its excellence that you can guess where it comes from.
The sour orange produces the best wood for archery; and the less
fruit it bears the better the wood will prove. It should be cut
before the fruit comes, or it will split.

Many of the praises I have sung of the orange-tree are also due
to the lemon-tree, with the exception of its wood not being so
tough or flexible, but stiffer and more brittle, and unfit for bows.
In perfume, both of flowers and leaves, it is even superior to the
orange-tree. In shade it is inferior: and the yellow and green of
its colouring, when the fruit is ripe, is inferior to the reddish gold
and dark green of the orange-tree. Medicinally, it has all the virtues of the orange, with a few additional ones. The juice, mixed
with melted butter, makes a sovereign ointment for herpes and
skin eruptions. The juices of lemons and of their aristocratic and
far more beautiful cousins, the limes, are anti-scorbutic. Because
of its use as such in the British Navy and Merchant Service, the
Americans use the word 'limey' to designate Englishmen, as the
old shanty they used to sing on the Black Ball Line reminds us:

> Says she 'You lime-juice sailor
> Now see me home you may',
> But when we reached her cottage door
> She unto me did say . . .
> 'My flash man he's a shellback
> With his hair cropped short behind,
> He wears a tarry jumper
> And sails on the Black Ball Line.'

The drinking of lime-juice as a corrective to too much salt pork
was compulsory in the English Navy and

> 'The clippers that fly the Black Ball'

but it was always on tap in other lines of the British Merchant
Service. When quinine ran out during the war, many of us
malaria patients got definite relief from eating lemons and limes.
I happened to be convalescing in a good place for them: I have
never seen such colossal lime-trees as in the forests of the Belgian

Congo between Albertville and Elizabethville; and I take it that this wonderful fruit originated from Africa. The Portuguese peasants who in swampy districts, like that of Alcacer do Sal, suffer from malaria, use the juice *hot* with coffee to produce perspiration and shorten the shivering fits of malaria. The peel is said by the Portuguese peasants to strengthen one's gums if chewed regularly. In spite of the fact that they are sometimes superstitious, I have found that the Portuguese peasants have a considerable knowledge of natural medicine. For instance, at my last medical examination by the British Ministry of War Pensions I was found to be seriously ill with diabetes, and I was told to go on a course of insulin as soon as I got home to Portugal. An English lady friend living at Sintra told me there was no need for insulin, if I only did as the peasants, and took a course of stewed periwinkle (roots, flowers, and all), a handful to a litre, boiled for ten minutes, and taken in a wineglass after each meal. This did the trick completely in a month, and I have taken several tests since, half-yearly, without the faintest trace of sugar in my blood.

The whole of the rainy side of Sintra range is covered with masses of periwinkle, which flowers for most of the spring and summer and has a second flowering in the late autumn. It is a plant that loves water, and is very hard to find on the rainless side of the serra where I am building my house. But there happened to be a big clump of periwinkle (the only one for miles around), which saved me the expense of a water diviner. 'Sink your well there,' said Tio Domingos, a bewhiskered and gnarly neighbour of mine with a big black stocking cap sticking two feet upright on his brows. He pointed to the clump of periwinkles. I had not blasted three and a half metres deep when the water rushed in and flooded the hole—divined for me by a peasant and a periwinkle! This saved the ten pounds a diviner would have cost me, though my friend Rob Lyle, the poet, doing 'amateur' divination, had also had the forked stick wrenched from his hand near there, and had shown me the spot. The only trouble was that he was at the top of the quarry, on the edge, and my well is at the bottom. It would have meant ten more metres!

A street in the fishing village of Nazare

Above—The vineyards of the Douro
Below—Treading the grapes for port wine

Picture

Before we stop talking about the delightful lemon-tree, let me tell you of a magical quality it possesses—almost a human characteristic—in that it is the most anti-bolshevik tree in the world. I defy any pro-bolshy or pro-anarchist writer, from Ilya Ehrenburg down to Sir Herbert Read or even my ex-enemy comrade and kinsman, the late George Orwell, to write about a lemon-tree without making a fool of himself—rather, without the lemon-tree making a fool of him. We know that Nature has it in for such people as Communists and shows them up every time, but if any tree is the product of art rather than of Nature (except in the Belgian Congo), it is the lemon-tree, and it treats with merciless irony all those poets who take its name in vain. For such poets 'the answer is always a LEMON!' Let us take just two examples of fifty I could quote. The South African bolshy poet, Uys Krige, who used to go all starry-eyed about the joys of the Russian regime in Hungary or Bulgaria, but always went to Spain or Portugal for his holidays, and never to the countries he raved so lyrically about, wrote a wonderful anti-Portuguese story about a poor old ill-treated proletarian woman in Portugal, whose only property was a flower-pot with a small lemon-tree in it, and whose only delight was to watch it bearing its one solitary fruit—*in the summer!!* This Afrikaans poet gave a wonderful talk about his deeds of derring-do in the International Brigade, but the Internationals themselves disowned him—as the lemon-tree had done before. When the head of the Overseas Department of the B.B.C. expostulated: 'But you were never there at all,' he replied 'Oh, yes! I was—in spirit.'

The other lemonizer who was in the Civil War in spirit was Sir Herbert Read. He also took a flying leap with a lemon-tree, in his Song for the Spanish Anarchists, in which he serenades the weirdest lot of bleary-eyed thugs it was ever my misfortune to come across in the following lines:

> The golden lemon is not made
> That grows on the green tree.
> A strong man with his crystal eyes
> Is a man born free.

C

When we relieved the heroic city of Huesca, Sertorius's old capital, we found the anarchist artillery had been in possession of the cemetery commanding the city, which they had blasted systematically into rubble. They had dug up most of the graves in order to prise the gold teeth out of the skulls. They had set up a brothel and a bar amongst the shrouds and skeletons, and were drumming with thighbones on coffin lids to the sound of the accordion and mouth-organs. I never set eyes on such hideous babooneries as they had committed there. A Spanish medical officer who was there explained that nearly all anarchists suffered from syphilitic G.P.I., and that it was the reason for their necrophily and for their always digging up corpses—as in the case of the buried nuns in Barcelona, exposing their naked corpses in the streets—amongst other macabre stunts. We took them entirely by surprise and made short work of them with cold steel. When they saw the uniform and heard the song of the Legion, *El Novio de la Muerte* (The Sweetheart of Death), they did not half start yelling for their mothers! I had hardly finished cleaning my bayonet on the grass when the front-line mail arrived with a Don R on a motor-bike and side-car. In my packet was an English newspaper with a letter from 'British Intellectuals' protesting at the treatment anarchists were receiving from both sides—for even the Reds had had enough of them by that time and shot over 40,000 of them! One of the signatories was my old room-mate, Aldous Huxley. Still, one can hardly blame him. He never stood a chance, having been brought up on the Piltdown skull, which I am told his grandfather not only posed for as a model, but actually constructed as a self-portrait! What surprised me was that ex-officers like Herbert Read were capable of slobbering over these subhuman yahoos and canine baboons. The answer to him was, of course, likewise a lemon.

> The golden lemon (yes!) is made!
> The pruning-hook, the hoe, the spade,
> Were rivals of Cellini's trade
> To smith this wonder from the tree,

because before it was pruned, manured, and watered by the Moors, the European lemon was a worthless thorny pulp, the vegetable equivalent of an anarchist, who requires plenty of attention from the pruning-hook, in the form of sabre and bayonet, if civilized society is to continue. Lemons, and men, are not merely spawned, they require the most careful cultivation, discipline, and control (in men, preferably self-control) from the day of their birth to that of their death.

Other crops besides oranges and lemons which are grown in Portugal are in the list that follows this paragraph. It is interesting to note the all-round increase in production during the last twenty-eight years of the present regime. It is the rice industry which is growing the quickest, but most crops have more or less doubled themselves, when they have not trebled themselves. Portugal is the biggest producer of cork in the world, and the fifth largest producer of olive oil. Most of the olive oil is used for the tinned fish industry, in which Portugal excels the rest of the world, as Spain excels the rest of the world in its fresh fish. You can get fresher and cheaper fish in a far-inland city like Madrid, where it is rushed by high-powered lorries, than in the fish-shops of Hull or Grimsby; but the tinned fish of Spain does not equal that of Portugal, where fish-canning has been brought to a fine art, especially in the case of skinless sardines. Only in two tinned products does Spain hold its own with Portugal: that is in the tinning of small octopuses in their own ink (*calamares en su tinta*) and of a small kind of sprat (*boquerones*)—which are truly delicious.

PRODUCTION

Wheat		*Maize*	
1925—3,454,933	quintais [1]	1925—4,866,293	hectolitres
1935—6,089,771	,,	1935—3,837,633	,,
1945—3,146,415	,,	1945—2,537,536	,,
1950—5,745,926	,,	1950—6,881,215	,,
1951—5,796,412	,,	1951—6,146,799	,,
1952—5,788,822	,,	1952—6,499,757	,,
1953—6,581,916	,,	1953—4,993,639	,,

[1] A quintai is 128 lb.

Rye		*Potatoes*	
1925—1,295,422 hectolitres		1925— 3,396,445 quintais	
1935—1,203,539	,,	1935— 5,127,960	,,
1945—1,220,668	,,	1945— 7,424,534	,,
1950—1,700,338	,,	1950—11,277,337	,,
1951—1,936,707	,,	1951—13,903,592	,,
1952—1,753,552	,,	1952—10,726,772	,,
1953—1,748,421	,,	1953—10,760,497	,,

Rice		*Wine*	
1925— 169,730 quintais		1925— 5,672,309 hectolitres	
1935— 577,430	,,	1935— 5,924,361	,,
1945— 444,827	,,	1945—10,167,282	,,
1950—1,210,344	,,	1950— 8,725,000	,,
1951—1,412,967	,,	1951— 9,490,000	,,
1952—1,406,696	,,	1952— 5,802,000	,,
1953—1,293,109	,,	1953—11,736,000	,,

Cork		*Olive Oil*	
1925— 565,341 quintais		1925— 427,224 hectolitres	
1935— 950,404	,,	1935— 537,629	,,
1945—1,500,260	,,	1945— 442,160	,,
1950— 961,490	,,	1950— 437,325	,,
1951—1,174,670	,,	1951—1,158,332	,,
1952—1,687,350	,,	1952— 570,896	,,
1953—1,758,850	,,	1953—1,329,720	,,

The Forestry Department of Portugal is one of the most advanced in the world. The forests are beautifully kept and almost every tree is registered. The pines are lopped in such a way that they grow slender and tall for masts. You do not have to go looking around for a fine mast in a Portuguese forest, as I did in France when I wrote my anthology piece, *Choosing a Mast*, after I had climbed about 2,000 feet up the mountains and had to lug the mast, dodging the *gardes-champêtres*, by devious paths at dead of night. In a Portuguese forest these beautiful oreads fairly chuck themselves at your head, as my beautiful compatriots, more hospitable and patriotic than virtuous, the Durban and Cape Town ladies, chucked themselves at the heads of the British soldiers during the war. You cannot walk a hundred yards in a Portuguese pine-forest without finding

A slender tree as vertical as noon,

and this is due to the Portuguese skill in pruning, which leaves only a little top-knot at the summit of the tree so that all the trees are stretching vertically to try to catch up with themselves.

When you think of the size of the Portuguese fishing fleets, and the amount of sail they carry; when you remember that their cod fleet of schooners alone is bigger than any similar rival outfit in the world; when you have seen those singing colonnades and pergolas of pine pass your doorstep every half-year, and then you visit the vast forest areas occupied by these silent virgin armies of vertical, nautically-minded dryads and oreads, all on tiptoe and ready to elope with their lovers, the winds—it makes you feel like an admiral inspecting whole companies of prospective re- cruits for the W.R.N.S. who are on the point of 'stripping for action', and waltzing away with that voluptuous motion that only a mast and a woman can sway with, when they are under the Æolian influence either of the thundering blue north-easter, or that of the human zephyr, Strauss of Vienna. The cork-tree also has its poetry, in spite of the fact that the Portuguese do not teach it, like their pines

To soar in the height with a shape of delight,
Uplifting their stems like the string of a kite.

Rather, I should think they prefer their cork-trees to be thick and heavy, than high and breezy. But these generous trees provide quite as much of the national wealth of Portugal as the wine they prevent from running out of barrels, bungs, and bottles. The Forestry Department checks up on every cork-tree, even in the wild forests, and it is only allowed to be stripped of cork every eight or nine years. You have to get permission to strip even the wild cork-trees on your property. Cork-stripping is a skilled trade. The cork-stripper is usually an itinerary worker in the wilder parts. He carries his axe with the zealous care, pomp, and majesty with which a Tikolosh or a Priapus carries his insignium of office. The blade is always tenderly sandwiched in a piece of split cork, and even when the stripper goes to sleep in the train he carries his axe like 'the soldier's best friend' (his rifle) either at the 'slope' or the 'present arms'. Cork-trees when newly stripped go the most extraordinary colour, which I can only describe as being a mixture of vermilion and chocolate. They support with their generous mast of acorns a subsidiary trade, that of swine-herding. Towards the Spanish border you will find a strange kind of pig, a blood relation of the wild boar, and of the pig of Braga and of Argyllshire, with a straight tail. Very nasty customers they are, too, though they are said to make excellent sausages. In the advance up the Portuguese border in 1936, during the Civil War, these pigs were always attacking and devouring the wounded. Men used to ask you to shoot them rather than leave them. But the swineherds of Elvas, Evora, and the bordering province of Estramadura (fed on pork and acorns) have always been famous for their valour. Nearly all the great land-fighting conquistadors came from between the towns of Trujillo in Spain and Evora in Portugal—Pizarro, Bareto, Cortes, Balbao, Amagro and a dozen others!

When through my army service I was disabled from agricultural labour, and had to 'work' (as they call it) on the B.B.C. on the 'literary advisory board'—the softest job I ever had (a corporal could do it!)—my one regret was that I could not grow my own wine and bread, which are the very principles of human life and freedom. Next to seeing sunny slopes covered with vines, I love to see big stretches of wheat, like those you see on the Sagra outside Toledo, or that big stretch of Masai wheat by the Athi River in Tanganyika, or the fields round Brecon in Wales, or some of those lowland wheatfields between Newcastle and

Edinburgh where they plough the straightest furrows I've ever
seen: or, best of all, when the corn has gone yellow, to see
horizons of it, as you rush over the prairies in the Wheat-King
Express, from Chicago to Milwaukie, and you begin to think the
whole world is made of bread, and that no one need go hungry
any more.

> For vast as ocean it expands,
> A huge Sahara made with hands,
> Whose waves are blood, whose sands are bread.

On my Quinta of Bochechos, near Sintra, where we had an inexhaustible water-supply and could irrigate the whole farm in
fifteen minutes, my wife and I had the delight of growing our own
bread on ten acres of virgin soil which we cleared of scrub, so that
the finest corn in the whole district, according to the Government
threshers at Varzea, was grown by us. The name of our farm—
Bochechos—which I had to abandon for reasons of health, as I
can no longer dig or plough, means 'gurgle' or 'gargle' farm;
some say it is called that from the four gurgling naiads of silvery
water that laughingly streak down to Beckford's beloved river,
which runs through the farm, and is called the River of the
Apples, because of all the fruit that is shed upon it by the overhanging fruit trees. I would have called it the River of the
Loquats and Lemons, because I have seen it, after a windy flood,
shoaling with golden loquats and lemons, as it rushed under
our ancient bridge, to throw them into the Atlantic, which returned them on the wave-fringe like a mile-long string of amber
beads.

Other people, amongst whom is my learned friend Herr
Doctor Professor Hartgenburch of Heidelburg, and also my ex-
motor-bike instructor and dear friend, Sergeant 'Blotto' Pfane,
an Englishman with a German name, of the Intelligence Corps
Motor Transport Yard at Winchester, both being ardent philo-
logists (one professional and the other amateur, but equally
earnest in the study of words), have traced the name of the farm
(where they are often my guests) not to our beloved silvery

water-nymphs and their gurgling laughter, but to the amount of
wine that is grown, gurgled, and gargled on the premises—as all
of us can solemnly swear and protest on the Bible, with our three
right hands raised above our heads, having partaken of it jointly
and regally at many a hearty 'bender', on the very spot! I can
add, too, as circumstantial evidence in support of this ingenious
thesis, that the last three tenants of this farm who preceded me all
died of drinking wine, at the respective ages of 114, 94, and 98!
No other reason could be given for their deaths.

It is a serious punishment to have to eat English chemical
bread after growing one's own, and getting it ground just to the
right 'wholeness' at the neighbouring windmill. My favourite
book is *Don Quixote*, and I have always loved windmills, though
all my 'windmills have turned to giants' and all my 'giants to
windmills', as my friend and fellow South African, the poet,
David Wright, points out in *Poetry London*. I even paid 100
escudos to do the complete circle hanging on to the sails, just to
see what it's like, but I was too heavy and they wouldn't go
round. My wife nearly fell down with laughing when I stuck,
twelve feet up in the air. The miller with the windmill, to whom
I take my corn to be ground every week, on whose sails I try to
take circular rides, and whom I help to adjust his grindstone to
grind my corn to the right 'wholeness' and huskiness, because
he is always grinding it soft, anæmic, and white for other customers, but brown and hard for me—is a sheer wonder! A
most generous and kindly man, *for a miller!* Most people who
drink as much as he does see 'pink elephants with revolving
teeth' (as the lighthouse-keeper at Cape Guardafui told me he
could see, when I had to go and knock him out, and tie him up,
with D.T.'s, in the last war, and shunt him off in the dhow to the
'looney bin' at Aden). But this fellow does not see any pink elephants. No fear! It's the other way round! Pink and green
elephants are always lining up, and peeping, and star-gazing at
HIM, in wonderment, fright, admiration, and astonishment. Yes!
queueing up in front of observatory telescopes just to get an
astronomical glimpse of him, and they crowd each other out

desperately trying to use their trunks as telescopes, just to get one little squint at him! You ought to see him, my dear reader! He can't even tie up his bootlaces because his nose gets in the way! His nose, or rather trunk, is of a fabulous description, prehensile, like a raspberry in texture, dipped in flour and infinitely prolonged—that accounts perhaps for the passionate interest taken in him by these visionary, long-snouted pachyderms which are always 'seeing' him. But he is the only charitable miller I ever met! Nearly all other millers have very bad reputations, from Chaucer's time to ours. But he is the only man whose conviviality has reversed the role of pink or green elephants, for he is not of the type who've known

> Either pink elephants or green,
> But rather by such beasts are seen,
> When they are feeling far from well
> And have weird nightmares of their own.

It is one of the few faults of this noble race, the Portuguese, that they drink more per head than any other people in the world, including Scots, Irish or American, but they've got it growing on their doorstep, and they can stand up to it better than most of us can. But on Sundays you can see some of them shepherding invisible sheep along the main roads, from side to side; so, on Sundays, you motorists should drive carefully in Portugal.

I have already sung the praises, in verse, of both those noble trees, the oread-pine, and that rather more portly strapping nymph, the olive, which is in danger of being superseded by inferior, quicker-growing, ignoble oil-sources such as the groundnut and the sunflower. The wild olive grows in all the forests I have ever seen south of Avignon or north of Cape Town. The sovereign of all oils and fats could be multiplied 1000% by flying out olive boughs from Spain, Portugal, Italy and Provence, and grafting them on to all those wild olives, say on Kilimanjaro, Meru, or Kenya, and all those strips of bush where it grows, right down to the Cape Province, from Lake Tana southwards, almost to Cape Town. I have never ceased to reiterate this. It could have saved the whole disastrous Ground-Nut Fiasco and brought in double as many millions as were lost on that idiotic 'scheme'. It is a far better product than butter, on which the English depend as a substitute. Compare the stench of an English barrack-room or troopship (which comes mostly from the feet—'toe-jam') with the scentlessness of Portuguese or Spanish ones. Compare the time wasted by English soldiers 'queueing up at the latrines', with the ease and quickness with which Portuguese and Spanish soldiers relieve themselves and make way for the rest, while the English go on squatting for hours, like broody hens (why, they even keep books and magazines in their lavatories!)—and you will see that the olive is the diamond of all oils and fats!

It takes ages to grow olive-trees. That is the disadvantage. But if you do so, your great grandsons will have wonderful friends, to feed them both with fuel, light, and liquid sunlight (and their descendants—for generations). We always keep a floating wick in olive oil in front of the statue of Our Lady of Fatima—you can see to read by it and it lasts a month. The floating wick that burned in Tullia's tomb (Cicero's favourite daughter) for 1500 years was only a bit of string stuck through a floating disk of cork in about a gallon of olive oil. The olive-tree is one of the masterpieces of the Creator, and I love it next to some of the acacias (jacaranda, Kaffirboom, flame-tree, and flamboyant, all of the fragrant, flowering-bean family), which, as a mere poet, I am forced to love for their useless feminine beauty; though perhaps I love more dearly the great singing pines, my Highland cousins and sisters, whom I have 'climbed'[1] and made love to in the dark and at the risk of life, off the 'Cape of Storms' itself, when their bosomy blouses of canvas were slatting into tatters, and the lightning served us symbolically for kisses, and

---

[1] If it's a daughter, bounce her on your knee,
   If it's a son, send the bastard off to sea.
   Bell-bottom trousers and a suit of navy-blue
   Teach him to climb the rigging as I climbed you!

the thunder for consummations! That was on the old *Pamir*, and the *Edda* and the *Herzogino*.

The wood of the olive has this advantage over all other woods —that it seasons the best. It becomes like iron after a long time, and is not so brittle as ebony. It is one of the treasures of this world. So is its fruit! So is its oil! It ennobles the human body, anointing the Olympian athletes for the tussle. Pigs are supposed to resemble us (anatomically) more than monkeys; and bears even more than pigs. (That's the latest 'science'.) But if you take olive oil for your nourishment you'll find your nearest zoological ancestors are only Anglo-Saxons whose climate does not give them a chance to get enough olive oil. Pop-Eye, the Sailor Man (that's me!), has monopolized olive oil for the time being, till you get sensible forestry commissions on to the colonies of Kenya, Tanganyika, and Rhodesia. Even the natives nearly burst with laughing—that the British fell forests on one side of the same mountain, to get rid of *tsetses*, while they are planting forests on the other side of the mountain for '*reafforestation*'. Bureaucracy! We're getting as fatuous as the Russians. It reminds me of the paper shortage under the Labour Government, when the pen-happy Civil Service clerks had all gone haywire with self-importance, and, *in one week, I had seventy-five most important documents, all redundantly repetitive, on luxury paper* stuck through my letter-box, to ask me, on behalf of the British Government, *to save paper*!! Is it any wonder that my British uniform, battle-dress, bush-hat, medals, with the pay-book in the bum pocket of the battle-dress (bearing witness to exemplary military conduct) have been bleaching and fraying, now almost unrecognizably, on the scarecrow in my wheat-field, ever since I was disabled and read of the suicidal 'benders' of Roosevelt and Churchill at Casablanca and Yalta. Today I only wear my Spanish medals and one Portuguese one on the right civilian side for life-saving at sea. I charge one escudo to British tourists who wish to come and see my scarecrow, rigged up in Chindit uniform, and guarding a now desolate wheat-field at Galamares, near Sintra. The local urchins have torn the silver medals off the ribbons, but the latter are still recognizable, though the nightingales, blackbirds, and jays have done their little piece of work in whitewashing it till it looks more like the pith-helmet of a Kiplingite Anglo-Indian polo-player than anything that ever belonged to me, though I can play polo, too.

CHAPTER THREE

On Wines

THE COURSE of the River Douro, or Duero as the Spaniards call it, terminates at Porto, whence the famous wine derives its name. When the Duero becomes the Douro, at the frontier of Portugal, it changes its character, and after winding through hundreds of miles of waste upland, in terrific ravines, dives deep down into one of the richest and most beautiful valleys in the world, part of which [1] has been terraced by the hands of men for many centuries, so as to make use of every spare inch of its precipitous sides, rising from its schistose base to the beetling granite crests, which protect the vines from the gales and storms that tear the summits. It is a river of torrential spates which have been known to engulf ships, as with a tidal wave, in Porto harbour.

Till it reached Portugal the river had passed through barren country of an unearthly and celestial beauty, yet of ineffable sorrow—the most haunted and haunting landscape I know, and one which inspired some of the finest poetry ever written. But when it crosses the border, the poetry materializes into a visible and potable form of lyrical elation, which it requires no erudition to appreciate, or knowledge of languages to understand. From the border to the Atlantic the Douro speaks, or rather sings, a universal language.

Not much is known of the early history of the world-wide port-wine trade, though it is supposed to owe its life to British merchants, who started shipments in 1678. But wine has been

[1] The transport of wine was chiefly done by boat. A waterfall cut off part of the potential wine-growing territory, till it was blasted and levelled in 1792. These vines were grown throughout the whole region now demarcated by the Government.

grown on the Douro since Roman times, and the elaborate intricacy of the terracing on the slopes is such that all of it could not
be recent. It is as ornate in detail as a mediæval cathedral. It
bewilders one with its glittering metallic foliage and the infinity
of its corrugations. It affects one's vision like the shimmering
skin of a Grevy's zebra (not the broad-striped, common zebra)
when he is shrugging the flies off in the sunlight and successions
of electric tremors flash swirling through the satin of his hide. It
appears to be the work of æons of erosion, reminding me vividly
of the famous Valley of a Thousand Hills, within sight of which I
was born, in South Africa. The metallic effect of the vines is due
to spraying with copper sulphates. The artificial contours of this
landscape are so much more conspicuous than the natural ones
(pronounced and imposing though the latter are) that they produce the illusion of being cœval with the river and the mountains
they indent, just as the infinite convolutions in the lobe of one's
finger, which they closely resemble in pattern, are coeval with the
finger itself.

The population of this part of the country, especially on the
northern bank, is more robust, devout, vivacious, and better-
looking than the people of the Tagus and the South. Most of the
transport is done by ox-waggon and by very imposing-looking
boats, known as *rabelos*, with tall dark square-rigged sails, and
beautifully-curved prows like the crescent moon painted in delightful hues and patterns and often, as on the ancient Egyptian
galleys, with eyes designed on the bows, as though to enable the
boat to see its way! I once belonged to a Gliding Club in Provence, where this ancient, but delightful superstition found expression in furnishing the last thing in modern gliders with two
beautiful Spanish-looking eyes with the most realistic fimbriation
of long, black lashes, and feathery, nobly-arching brows. Some
of us almost fell in love with it, not only for its suave and voluptuous undulations, but for those eyes!

Wine has been grown on the Douro for local and neighbouring
consumption for more than 2,000 years. The vines were originally planted on the slopes most exposed to sunlight, in order to

fertilize the rich sweet wines favoured from early times to the end of the Middle Ages. This exclusive choice of sunlit space limited the area of cultivation to a part of that cultivated today. The stone tanks, or *lagares*, in which the wine was trodden seldom exceeded five pipes, and this required very much smaller vats than those used nowadays. Today the *lagares* vary from twenty to fifty pipes.

It was not till 1703 that Portugal signed the Methuen Treaty with Great Britain, upon which shipments at once increased. From Regua, where the schist (so necessary to the port-wine grape) begins, vine cultivation spread up the valleys of the Douro and its tributaries till the whole vast region became, almost exclusively, a wine-producing one.

The wine-growers, however, were for a long period at the mercy of the shippers, who dictated the prices. Much ill-feeling was caused by low prices, and this finally led to a political crisis. The Marquis de Pombal, then virtually the Dictator of Portugal, with a view to restraining the avarice of the shippers on the one hand, and the unscrupulousness of the growers (who grew vines in unsuitable places) on the other, finally founded the "General Company of Viniculture in the Upper Douro". It was known to the English as "The Royal Oporto Wine Company". The famous Marquis granted this company certain royal prerogatives in 1756.

An era of comparative prosperity succeeded the dangerous crisis which had threatened the port-wine trade; nevertheless too many red-tape restrictions were imposed by the company. Wines for shipment could be bought only in certain specified areas. Though the Marquis had meant well, the wines had to be tasted and approved for shipment: and this led to favouritism, bribery, and corruption of tasters and other employees. Trade to certain Brazilian states, hitherto good customers, was curtailed as a reprisal for certain Customs restrictions imposed by them on other Portuguese exports. In 1834, after seventy-eight years of mainly beneficial, if partly detrimental influence, the company was dissolved, and free trade was allowed because of the ideas which were

belatedly percolating through to Portugal from France of that
very doubtful blessing—the Revolution. As a result, the trade
was almost ruined a second time, because the quality of both the
wine and brandy deteriorated as a consequence of this unbridled
licence. All kinds of synthetic hooch were passed off as Portuguese
produce. The name of port suffered in its prestige. The Government, yielding to an ultimatum on the part of the growers, re-
instated the company, which, however, proved to be incapable of
rectifying the chaos arising from over-production. All rights and
privileges granted to the company were therefore again with-
drawn. It seemed as if by the repetition of these contrary
manœuvres the whole industry was perpetually 'leaping out of
the frying-pan' into a more uncomfortable temperature. But the
two principles, however bad they were in themselves, were
mutually corrective—like counter-poisons. Entire freedom of
trade was granted again in 1865. Heaven knows what might have
happened. But at this very juncture the Devil himself intervened
as an involuntary benefactor, in the shape of that dread scourge,
the phylloxera. By desolating many vineyards, it counteracted
the curse of over-production, and thus the industry weathered
another crisis, but only just. It was not till 1907 that João
Franco, then Premier, demarcated the Douro Region as it remains to this day, and granted to the city of Oporto the exclusive
right of the shipment of Douro wines over the bar of the Douro
River.

That was a great step in the right direction, and since then the
industry has flourished. The Nationalist Government took over
the supervision and fiscalization of the trade in 1932. Finally a
Port Wine Institute was founded—an official State Department,
dedicated to the scientific and economic improvement of the industry. The State reserves the role of mediator in all discussions
of the interests at stake. It controls the duties of fiscalization, and
supervises the tasting of all the wines exported from the city of
Porto. The efficiency of this expert organization ensures that all
wine shipped from Porto is produced in the Douro Region and is
a genuine wine of guaranteed quality.

Barco rabelo on the Douro

Above—Campinos

Casa de Portug

Below—Hayloads being carried under the cork trees

It appears that the original motive for taking wine aboard British ships at Porto was to provide anti-scorbutic vitamins for crews who subsisted mainly on salt pork. It has taken the human race its whole existence up till now to learn that the oceans themselves provide everything necessary to counteract scurvy. However, there is no more pleasant way of counteracting it than by drinking good wine. It is certainly better than sucking raw fish, as Bombard did when he crossed the Atlantic in his rubber dinghy.

From the Fleet and the Merchant Service in the English seaports, the taste for port seems to have rapidly filtered ashore, and it was not long before it became the ceremonial drink of mayors and aldermen, and the convivial after-dinner drink of the squirearchies, and the upper middle class in general, throughout the United Kingdom, where, as if in commemoration of its medicinal qualities, it is often served in tiny glasses, as if it were a medicine!

The glass for port wine should be a large tulip-like one, a little narrower, if anything, round the brim than round the middle, so as to retain the perfume: it should be a thin glass, so that the warmth of one's hand can arouse, in response to its caress, the exhalation of the full fragrance of the soul of the wine. In a full tiny glass it 'wastes its sweetness on the desert air', for it cannot then be fondled and gently awakened so as to kindle an amorous reaction. The drinking of port is analogous to good horsemanship, which, in its turn, is analogous to the act of love. It requires skill, practice, and experience. A fiery horse under an unpractised rider will never show forth its full mettle, nor will a beautiful woman beneath a rough, clumsy lover. But the minute a true horseman bestrides a fine horse, the latter will arch his neck and begin high-stepping with pride in his own beauty, and in the mastery with which he is managed: the same with a woman: and the same with port wine.

A good drinker will similarly, in the preliminary ritual, rouse the mettle of the wine before he tastes it. Priests are often exquisite connoisseurs of port. Otherwise, fully to appreciate good port, if one is not religious, one should simultaneously have

D

something in one of a poet and a passionate lover (which are synonymous). Caressing the breast of the Muse, which the glass should resemble not only in shape, but in sensitivity to a subtle caress, one sets fire to her blood, which is the wine. Then comes the kiss! The kiss should be long drawn, slow, and infinitely tender: not one of those 'smacking kisses'. One 'smack-kisses' beer, *vin ordinaire*, *vino corriente*, or *vinho correnta*, which in the realm of femininity are represented by strapping A.T.S. sergeants, barmaids, land-girls, and bosomy bus-conductresses. One does not bite or smack-kiss the Muses, which in the realm of femininity represent vintage port and other good wines. One kisses them tenderly, reverently, yet passionately, as a bridegroom kisses his bride on the first night: as hawk-moths, humming-birds, and sunbirds, hovering in mid-air, kiss the flowers from which they extract the nectar with their long, thrilling tongues: or as bees kiss the erected pistil of the open hibiscus-flower, without bruising it or even bending it. One does not swallow port straight down. It should first penetrate every pore of one's palate and tongue, which latter is as important in the osculation of wine as of women, being one of the most sensitive organs of one's body. The animals that would appreciate port the best, and if they had any intelligence would make the best port wine-tasters of all, would be, first of all, the terrible but lovely black-and-green mambas of Africa, and the great king-cobras of Asia, for these snakes are the wariest, the most sensitive to sound, and the most enchantable by music of all animals, and, being earless, hear entirely with their supersensitive tongues. (That is why they are always flicking them out like radio-antennae.) I notice that Ditmars says that it is a superstition that snakes can be lured, hypnotized, and charmed by music. His doubt is the usual scepticism of the closet-biologer. (I used to catch snakes for the Durban Zoo, and found them susceptible to a guitar.) He is a great expert on venoms and serums, but knows nothing about the catching of snakes before they arrive at his clinic, when they are already lethargic and tone-deaf from confinement. The professional snake-catchers, snake-killers, and snake-charmers rely chiefly on sound effects to lure snakes from their holes and lairs. If one could catch the sound of the slightest rustle of a leaf on one's tongue, as a mamba can, it is interesting to speculate how one would enjoy the vibrations and waves issuing from the more substantial music, which is a good wine, if one's tongue was gifted with such supersensitiveness as a snake's. Still, as Pope points out in what is one of the finest lines in English poetry, if our senses were commensurate with our intellects, we would not be able to bear the excruciating intensity of our pleasures, and might

> Die of a rose in aromatic pain.

The greatest enemy of wine-tasting is nicotine, the blunter of sensitive tongues and palates: and the proof of this is that to the most sensitive tongues in the world—those of snakes—nicotine is as deadly a poison as prussic acid is to us, or as cobra venom once it gets under the skin (for one can swallow a pound of it without harm provided one's mouth is intact, without cuts or abrasions). One drop of nicotine on the tongue of the largest boa-constrictor or anaconda will fulminate it as suddenly as if one had bashed its brains out with a sledge-hammer.

There lived a gentleman in London who drank a pint of the best port every night, and as a consequence lived to be ninety-something. As a lawyer, he rivalled the very snake of Eden in the persuasive eloquence of his tongue, due no doubt to its sensitivity to port wine and to constant lubrication with it. One of his guests, one of the 'bright young things' of today, who show no respect for ceremony, ritual, or tradition, asked him if he might smoke while the port was going on its round. Amidst the horror-stricken silence that ensued, 'Certainly', spluttered the irate nonagenarian. Then, turning to the butler, he ominously added: 'James, bring Mr. X a cigarette, and his hat and coat.'

In the opinion of Senhor Valente-Perfeito, who has written most of the best books on port wine, and one in English, *Let's Talk About Port* (published by the Port Wine Institute), nicotine undoubtedly is the Enemy No. 1, not only of wine, but also of food, because it anæsthetizes the senses of taste and smell.

Having given up smoking the better to enjoy the gifts of God, which are wine, bread, and other food, I find the sacrifice has been more than compensated, for now I can even taste and enjoy water, a thing I could never have even imagined when I was a smoker. I grow my own wine and bread, and I find that without nicotine I can even enjoy dry bread, as a Spanish peasant enjoys it, and I can name the particular fountain or well (there are six on my farm) whence my '*caseiro*' has drawn my drinking-water, just from its taste. I could never have done this before. In the opinion of Senhor Valente-Perfeito, 'an inveterate smoker' himself, the appreciation of light types of wine is not incompatible with smoking, but he adds: 'Vintage wine, in general, and vintage port, in particular, are entirely out of the question so far as smoking is concerned.' Later on, however, he relents a little and says: 'The rule is for one to abstain from smoking till the decanter has gone round twice.'

Just as there are agents such as nicotine which blunt one's perception of the true soul of a good wine, so there are agents which sharpen that perception, enhance the fragrance, and emphasize the flavour of wine. These are the sharp-tasting, bitter-sweet '*marmalada*' or quince jelly; the cheese of the Serra (*Queijo da Serra*) made of sheep's milk; or the ordinary tart goat's-cheese that one finds everywhere in Portugal.

Though the waterfalls and rapids of the Cachão de Valeira which had hindered the expansion of the wine-growing area were finally blasted and levelled in 1792, after sixteen years of hard work, thus liberating a region of a similar mesological stratum to that already planted, and of identical soil, the active transport by boats of port wine from above the levelled rapids did not begin till 1807. It was found that this soil of Cambrian and Pre-Cambrian schist extended almost to the Spanish frontier, and its inclusion (as early as 1849) in the demarcated 'region' is fully justified today. This soil owes its chief value to the flaking of schist rock which acts as a corrective to the excess of clay. It is rich in potassium (12%), but lacks nitrogen, lime, and organic substances.

Meteorological conditions also contribute to the special character and mettle of the wine. There is plenty of evidence, in the shape of dried wells and the vestiges of old orchards, that the rainfall was once heavier than it is now. This made the reafforestation of the summits imperative, and it has been carried out with skill and determination. The rain runs too easily, without encountering any pockets, off the steep rocky hillsides: and in the more barren parts a thousand vines will yield only one pipe of wine, though such wine is of a far higher quality than that which grows in the lusher parts of the region, where there are springs of water, and where a thousand vines will yield up to four or five pipes. These are the hollows in the hillsides where they rise from the river, and where not only olives, figs, and almonds can flourish, but where oranges and lemons can sometimes be grown. Yet, for all that, the one pipe of the veritable blood of Pegasus, yielded by the thousand vines on the barren crags, is both a Parnassian and Olympian beverage, an ethereal nectar, worth more than all the five pipes yielded by the thousand vines in the greener parts, plus the yields of a thousand olive, fig, almond, orange, and lemon-trees in the lower valleys. It would not be the first time that Highland valour, or, to put it more literally, the *blood of the Highlands*, has triumphed over superior numbers.

Hailing from America, the home of prohibition, the phylloxera insect—the pussyfoot of the animal kingdom—is the worst enemy of the vine. So American vines, which are more resistant to the pest, had to be imported and planted. The American stock is planted first, then the Portuguese vine is grafted on to it. This caused the quality of the wine to deteriorate, but only slightly. Yet we may never hope to taste again the crowning glories of the best pre-phylloxera vintages of the first half of the nineteenth century.

In this precipitous region, next to the phylloxera, the force of gravity constitutes the worst enemy of the vine and the vine-growers. Aided by the wear and tear of contraction and expansion, caused by the extremes of temperature, which range from below freezing point in winter to 115° F. in the shade in summer,

the precipitous angle of the slopes induces landslides of col-
lapsing terraces which avalanche sometimes from the very top-
most terrace to the base, tearing out the roots of the vines as they
go. Vine-growing in this region is an epic struggle, the perpetual warfare of a tough and hardy population against hostile
natural conditions—terracing, manuring, liming, reafforestation,
and cultivation. There is none of the idyllic pastoral atmosphere
of the Côte d'Or on the banks of the Saône in Burgundy, where a
vast lime deposit was so obligingly laid on by prehistoric men in
the shape of the bones of millions of wild horses, with a sprinkling
of aurochs and bison, which, for thousands and thousands of
years, they drove in from the surrounding country up the
Solutré mountain. This mountain narrows, as it rises gradually,
from a wide base to a high precipitous wedge, over which the
panic-stricken animals would force each other in headlong
avalanches, to plunge to their death; then they were cut
up by the vast population which settled at the base of this
convenient *abattoir*, distributing the skulls and bones of the horses
for miles around. This prehistoric Chicago seems to have been
organized on a scale as colossal as its modern replica, and to have
supported as vast a population as the four million hefty, chop-fed,
magnificently hospitable citizens of the City of Ares,[1] the Queen of
the Prairies. From the point of view of poetic inspiration, burgundy is superior to port, though it is less warming to the heart
and less flattering to the palate, and I cannot help attributing this
fact to the percentage of wild horse that canters away with one's
spirit while drinking that lighter, more natural, unfortified wine.
Not in vain was poetic inspiration represented as a winged horse,
and Hippocrene, the 'horse-fountain' of prophecy and song, as
having sprung from a kick of his hoof. Bordeaux and Rioja are
also great poetic inspirers: the former being the only wine that
does not harm one when taken in large quantities.

Since no considerate cave-men limed the soil for the inhabitants
of the Douro valley, a great deal of hard work has to be done to

[1] Chicago is not only the chief meat-producing city in the world but is also
the generous capital of the world's richest wheat-belt.

fertilize it. Everything has to be done by human hands, since mechanical aid and ploughing are more or less precluded by the steepness of the mountain-sides. The hardest work is the walling of the terraces, so as to hold the soil level and keep it from being swept away by the rains. The cost of planting and cultivation is therefore probably higher than in any other viticultural district in the world.

The planting is done either with a crowbar, or with a double-tongued hoe or pick. It is a cross between a pick and a hoe. The hole has to be several feet in depth. When the double hoe is used, none of the roots are stripped from the stock. But in difficult ground, where only a narrow hole can be made with a crowbar, nearly all the roots are taken off, to prevent entanglement and mutual strangulation. Whenever the planted American stock sprouts a tendril, it is removed, and only the grafted Portuguese vine is allowed to make any headway above ground. A shallow trench is dug round each vine. Manuring is done at long intervals. Beans or lupins are grown, and ploughed or dug into the soil while they are still in flower.

In Spring the vines have to be sulphured and sprayed with a solution of lime and copper sulphate, which gives the vineyards their bright, metallic, azure tint.

The vintage sometimes starts at the end of September, but generally in October, when the grapes have ripened to their full maturity.

An army of men, women, and children swarms into the Douro region from neighbouring regions, in gangs which have been contracted previously. They come dancing along to the accompaniment of pipes, guitars, concertinas, and drums. The aged people and the children pick the grapes and put them into small baskets, from which they are transferred to larger ones, which the stronger men carry on their shoulders to the stone tanks (*lagares*), where they are trodden and allowed to ferment.

In spite of mechanical progress, the naked human foot has never been improved on for crushing the grapes yet leaving the skins, pips, and stems unbruised and intact. When the men have washed their feet, with arms linked, to prevent each other from slipping and falling, they prance singing knee-deep from one end of the tank to the other; after which they separate, when the foothold becomes surer. All this work is done as if it were *not* hard labour, in a spirit of revelry and jubilation which makes our hoppickers seem glum by comparison. It is tremendously hard work, and only the very strongest men can do it. In the Latin-Catholic countries—Provence, Spain, Italy, Portugal, and Gascony—the people take the greatest delight in their work and in their religion, which are regarded as sources of the greatest pleasure, rather than as trials, tribulations, hardships, and inflictions, as in Protestant countries. A religious festival in Marseilles, Rome, Toulouse, Bordeaux, Madrid, Barcelona, Seville, Porto, or Lisbon, is an occasion for music, rejoicing, and revelry. A Sunday is not only a day of rest, but of festivity and recreation.

The vintage lasts from a fortnight to three weeks. After being trodden for the first time, the musk or grape-juice is allowed to rest till the morrow, when they work it over again. The addition of 20% of wine brandy fortifies the wine, and by counteracting fermentation, preserves the natural sugar which gives the wine its sweetness. In ordinary, sourish wine the sugar has nearly all been fermented into alcohol.

The wine is drained off into large casks, generally holding about 550 litres, and carted by bullock-waggon down to the river-side, whence the boats take it down to Vila Nova de Gaia, where the merchants mature it. The bullocks in this region wear a very picturesque head-yoke of leather. Years of oxidization in wooden casks eventually produce the beautiful topaz colour in the wine. More and more wine is being carried by the railway nowadays, though the river is still the main thoroughfare. The flat-bottomed boats are easy to cast off, difficult to capsize, and easy to manage in the rapids, by reason of the immense leverage of their rudders.

On reaching Gaia the wine is carted to vats, which sometimes hold 200 pipes, where they are blended into the standard, uniform port wine. It is in the ninth year that the wine begins to beautify its colouring and breathe forth the aroma for which it is famous. It will by then have lost some of its alcoholic strength and will have to be fortified with a much older brandy, of an age suitable to the requirements of its own old age.

The wine of an exceptionally good year is not blended, but kept apart, and that is what the English call a *Vintage Port*.

Port is essentially a wine for a cold, damp climate, and for peoples who subsist on cereal drinks and cider. As a result of recent propaganda drives, I am told, the Portuguese have begun to take some interest in port as a drink, and not merely an agricultural product for export. But the three million inhabitants of Norway drink far more port between them than is drunk by the nine million Portuguese, who drink natural, unfortified wines *with*, not *after*, their meals. I have never drunk port in Portugal, nor even seen anyone drinking it, though I have seen bottles of it in bars in Lisbon, Estoril, Praia da Rocha, and other resorts frequented by English people. I learned to enjoy port in its proper setting—that is to say, with the Fellows of Colleges at Oxford, Cambridge, and Trinity (Dublin). In Scotland and the United States I always drink whisky, which is the absolute monarch of all drinks, and that which, with bordeaux wine, is most indulgent to one's health. Kentucky is the whisky paradise of the world, but American beer is execrable. Fortified wines (port, malaga, madeira, marsala, sherry, etc.) are generally avoided by the people of the countries that produce them. Sherry is the exception: Spaniards, though a sober people, drink almost as much as they export, which is a great deal. Madeira is also drunk by the people of that island, though to a lesser extent.

The present condition and composition of standard blended port were determined and dictated by the shippers in catering for English tastes: and this is a great credit to English tastes, since port wine is loved and venerated throughout the world, in all those countries which are not too warm for the enjoyment and healthy ingestion of a sweet, fortified wine. Heat, and even warmth of climate, are hostile to the consumption of the strong wines and sugars of which they are so prolific. Whisky is the only strong drink which is not fatal in the tropics. But in the cold, rainy climates of the North the glowing, sunny southern soul of the strong wine sings to the human heart, in the words of that noble poem of Baudelaire, *The Soul of the Wine*, which I have translated thus:

> One night the wine was singing in the bottles,
> 'Mankind, dear waif, I send to you, in spite
> Of prisoning glass and rosy wax that throttles,
> A song that's full of brotherhood and light.
>
> 'I know that toil and pain and sweat you thole,
> Under the roasting sun on slopes of fire,
> To give me life and to beget my soul—
> So I will not be thankless to my sire,
>
> 'Because I feel a wondrous joy to dive
> Down, down the throat of some work-weary slave.
> His warm chest is a tomb wherein I thrive
> Better than in my subterranean cave.
>
> 'Say can you hear that rousing catch resound
> Which hope within my beating heart sings high?
> (With elbows on the table crowd around,
> Contented hearts, my name to glorify.)
>
> 'I'll light the eyes of your delighted wife.
> I'll bring your son both rosy health and muscle,
> And be to that frail athlete in this life
> Like oil that primes the wrestler for the tussle.
>
> 'In you I fall, ambrosia from above,
> Sown by the hand of the Eternal Power,
> That poetry may blossom from our love
> And rear to God its rare and deathless flower!' [1]

[1] From *The Poems of Baudelaire* translated by Roy Campbell.

CHAPTER FOUR

Under the Atlantic

THE FIRST submarine fishing on the Portuguese coast is to be had at the Berlengas islands, seven or eight miles off the coast. Motor-boats can be hired at Peniche, and there is a regular ferry-boat twice a day. One has to take one's own food and bedding. The trip takes an hour and a quarter in good weather. The Berlengas are granite rocks and go down pretty steeply, so that you get big fish close in-shore—*corvinos*, tunnies, bass, *bonitos*, ribbon-fish, and of course groupers, which is a corruption of the Portuguese name, *Garupa*. Amongst the crevasses in the rocks are swarms of crayfish and octopus. The underwater landscape is luxuriant, consisting of submarine ravines shaggy with bright waving seaweed. In fact these islands swarm with life, both above the water-line and beneath it. I have never seen so many rabbits in my life, and the land vegetation is as weird and beautiful as the seaweed. In the deeper water are big shoals of *pargo* and *pargo mulatto*, two varieties of red sea-bream.

As I have never 'frogged' in British waters, I do not know how many dangerous fish British frogmen are wise to. I have never seen the deadly black-and-yellow sea-snake under Spanish or Portuguese waters, but as I killed one as far north as Tangier, it is just possible that a stray one might cruise to the only warm water on the Portuguese coast, which is on the strip of coast between Cape St. Vincent and Trafalgar. This snake is as deadly as a mamba, a king cobra, or hideous, Picasso-blue Gaboon viper, which last is the only one of the viper, adder, or rattlesnake family to be able to inject nerve-venom, though it also injects, at the same time, 50% of blood-venom. There is no serum for sea-snake venom, as far as I know,[1] so if you get a 'peck' from one of these customers you have about six minutes to live—or rather to die. It is easy to recognize—a flickering ribbon of greased lightning, bisected laterally with black on top and yellow underneath.

Everyone, of course, knows not to meddle with a sting-ray or a moray. The moray is pugnacious. It has a poisonous bite, but its venom is a weak form of the kind of blood poison injected by adders, vipers, and rattlers. It works, not through the nerves, but the circulation. The history of the moray is worth recording. It is not generally known that the moray is a superb delicacy. The ancient Romans knew it all right. But we in South Africa, and Britons all over the world, throw them away because of our associating them with venomous bites. But venomous bites have nothing to do with food-poisoning: only last month I travelled back to Lisbon from New York with a Miss Etelvina Pereira as my table-companion, a young Portuguese lady, and a professional circus rider, who delighted me, not only because I also have been a circus-rider, but with the information that her father, the owner of nineteen performing elephants, had just started a rattlesnake cannery in California, in response to a growing popular relish for rattlesnakes. Once a moray's head is off it is as wholesome a delicacy as any in the sea. Salted it dries easily in the sun and can be preserved indefinitely.

How much the Romans appreciated them not only as food, but as pets, can be seen by the frequency with which the human surname of Murena (always a rich man) crops up in Roman history and literature. Murena means moray (that is our corruption of the French word *murine*). Romans always went by a nickname concerned with their trade or with some physical peculiarity or mental characteristic, and these names often stuck to families, like our trade-names Smith, Fletcher (which in its turn means Arrowsmith), Archer, Carpenter, etc. A man who was called Murena

[1] I tried mamba-serum on an Indian at Sezela about a minute after he was bitten. It is nerve-poison serum but he died all the same, though I sucked the bite on his ankle.

would derive his name (and vast fortune) from trading in murenas. That enormous fortunes were made in this trade can be seen to this day, for instead of liking turkey for Christmas and other fêtes, the Italians still insist on having eels—congers and morays —and they even prefer their bread in whigmaleerie formations, that is to say in the form of spaghetti, macaroni, and vermicelli, being the greatest twist-and-twiddle experts on this earth. So also they prefer their fish in macaroni formations, as eels, needle-fish, ribbon fish, congers, and (above all) as morays. Even their beautiful (perhaps slightly over-ornate) language is twirlier and twiddlier than a bunch of vermicelli on its way from the plate to the mouth of an Italian. (Mine always falls back on the plate.) Their modern architecture seems to follow the same pattern as their food and their speech.

We will treat Enemy No. 1 of frogmen first—the moray, and end up with the minor enemies, sharks, jellyfish, weevers, sea-scorpions, etc. A whole book could be written on the subject of the moray eel and its rôle in the decline of the Roman Empire. (Every rich Roman household kept one.) Cassius, the traitor, had a huge one. He said it was the only friend he had in the world, except his dupe Brutus, both of whom Dante, quite rightly, dumps in the most highly sulphuretted and malodorous part of his Inferno, along with Judas Iscariot. He had this moray fixed up with earrings and a necklace of rubies, diamonds, sapphires, and emeralds. We know from Seneca in his essay *De Ira* (*Concerning Wrath*), and also from Pliny the Younger, that Aulus Fedeus had another, the biggest on record, a man-eater, about the size of a full-grown python, in a glass tank: it had one of the finest *rivière* (river) necklaces in Rome wound four times round, and huge pearl pendants hanging from its gill-fins, by way of earrings. In those days even Colchester oysters produced pearls the size of pigeons' eggs, so it must have been a very beautiful necklace indeed (what a waste!), after the style of that necklace or *rivière* of pearls, which a mistress of a millionaire baron was wearing at a dinner in Paris, when it became unclasped at the back of her swan-like neck: and glided down between her lovely bosoms to regions even more theoretically tantalizing: thereby doubling its value, by eliciting this priceless jewel of a remark in a loud whisper from my friend, the late Sir Ronald Storrs: 'It's the first time I've seen a *river* flowing *towards* it's *source*!'

This horrible and stupendous moray belonging to Aulus Fedius was fed chiefly on recalcitrant slaves, who were thrown into the tank naked and alive, to be attacked by the fangs of the monster, and devoured before the gloating eyes of the sub-human who was its owner, and his family of ghouls. On one occasion a nervous slave broke a valuable dish at the very moment when Augustus Cæsar was a guest in this house. He was 'sentenced to the moray', but, breaking away from those who were about to heave him into the tank, he rushed to Augustus and, prostrating himself, asked for any other death than that of being eaten by the moray. Augustus granted his request.

The exaggerated love of animals (especially of morays) is almost always a sign of vicious misanthropism and cruelty. Cassius's dumb-chum, the moray, adored him and would rear up out of the water to be fondled as soon as he recognized the approach of his master, whom he knew by sight, by his voice and probably by the moral stench that must have been their spiritual bond.

The decadent Clodia was capable of poisoning her husband and committing incest with her brother, yet she was inconsolable for the death of a sparrow!

Whenever an empire is on the wane, its decline is symptomized by an exaggerated love of animals. Cambyses conquered Egypt by driving a lot of cats, billy-goats, dogs and jackasses in front of his army, so that the Egyptian archers dared not shoot for fear of hurting the animals. If a parachute army wanted to conquer modern Britain they would only have to land with poodles and pekes in their arms: and no one would fire a shot!

Now it may be that the would-be fisherman of morays or self-defender against them will be curious to know why, in captivity, the old Roman pet morays and congers could grow to the size of a python, as thick as your thigh, and be able to devour a man without leaving a trace in a glass tank. You can double the weight and size of any eel by artificial feeding. If you are staying in Portugal and, on your undersea prowl, you locate the lair of a moray or a conger, do not be in a hurry. That eel has an address just like your London office. He spends at least three-quarters of his time or more in his office. He does not have to go abroad to secure his prey, any more than a lawyer or a psychotherapist does. Their prey *comes* to them—and to the moray. When you find where a moray or a conger lives, beg or buy all the offal from the hotel where you are staying and dump it outside his office or consulting-room. In two weeks he will be much bigger, and twice as worth while shooting.

The moray will almost invariably let you get quite close up to his head as long as his body is in his hole. The killing of a moray with an underwater gun is safe if, in the case of a lateral shot, the point of the dart is kept well within the muzzle of the spring-gun. The moray will first of all try to get back into his hole, pulling the dart with him: if he succeeds in getting some way in, and expands his ribs, snake-fashion, inside his tunnel, nothing will ever get him out, even if his head is pulled clean off. But if the dart, having transfixed him, is kept rigidly still, and the fisherman also keeps still, the eel will come out of his hole and wrap himself round the dart in an effort to break it. Then you can surface at once: wrapped round the dart, he will be infinitely more preoccupied with it than with the swimmer. Even in land-hunting, the assegai and the arrow, in the case of dangerous animals, have this one great advantage over firearms. Struck with a bullet, a lion or a grizzly is unable to identify it, and may charge the hunter. But struck with an arrow, he sees the shaft protruding and feels as if it is *attacking* him, so that for a brief while at least it will preoccupy him to bite and claw the arrow, before he turns on the hunter, as he will in the long run if he does not at first. If the swimmer approaches the moray frontally, there is an even more certain and deadly way of killing him. If the arrow-head is slowly rotated in narrowing circles, the moray will follow it with his eyes until it has come within an inch of his lip. He will then, out of curiosity, put out his head and nip the point with his mouth. You can then transfix him lengthwise from head to tail, a paralysing shot, which prevents him from swelling his ribs out in his hole, since he will rather be compressing his body on the shaft, inwardly, to try to eject it.

These are the only two fish in the sea,[1] except a basking shark, which will approach you, when you approach them—unless you consider an octopus a 'fish'. I used to think the octopus, because it can be dangerous, was hostile: but its very playfulness (which is amorous) is unsafe. But if it makes advances to you, tickle it. It will then leave go of the rock to which it is attached and begin holding you with all its feelers and you can kick up to the surface, when it will let go. I was nearly drowned in 1930 when, owing to primitive self-made equipment and bad visibility, I mistook the metal beak of the now famous sunken galley at Fos (from which I was the first to fetch up the *amphoræ*) for a stone building, before it collapsed. It was held together by barnacles and mussels in those days, which made me think it was a stone temple when I swam into the broken bows and was embraced by a playful octopus of five and a half kilos.

I can dismiss the octopus in these few words. It will not, like all other fish or molluscs, swim away from you if you swim towards it—a manœuvre that will take the kick out of the charge of the hugest and most voracious shark in the world, even when it is charging at you at forty miles an hour. A Blue Pointer which could swallow an ox—Tiger-Lamia, the most deadly animal machines ever created, next to the mambas, cobras, and killer-whales—will flinch and swerve if whatever it is chasing does not accelerate as it approaches. So will any other carnivorous fish. If you slack off trolling a mullet when a shark rises to it, the latter loses interest and swerves away. To scream into one's face-mask will scare away a shark.

Now the octopus, though a mollusc, is of a far higher intellect than any fish. (Fish are reflexive and only stimulated by flight.)

[1] The conger does not have a venomous bite, but he'll take off a finger without winking.

An octopus looks you in the eyes. If one of them has been surprised by low tide and he is trying to creep past you to the deep
water, he will 'freeze', like a lion or an antelope, till you look away
again, then he will reach out his long elastic feelers and heave
himself another foot or so, till you look at him again. The small
ones are good to eat, but you have to thump the big ones with a
rolling-pin for a long time before they become tender.

If the population of the world goes on increasing in proportion
to soil-erosion, the ultimate diet of the world will have to be
plankton seaweed and octopus: and I suggest for English people,
overcrowded, congested, and unimaginative, that they learn to
stomach the octopuses (in their ink) that swarm on their shores.[1]
If they can stomach the poisonous, racially suicidal ink of their
own journalists, they ought to be able to learn the ingestion of the
more salubrious ink of an octopus.

The warning I give to the inexperienced frogman, in Portuguese waters is this: swim towards a shark, *unless* it is a plankton-
feeding basking-shark, because these latter are sissies—they are
eaten up with curiosity and they even try to make love to wooden
boats, capsizing the crews. I had one of those whale-sized ones of
the Indian Ocean, about forty feet long, carrying my dhow on his
back for about twenty yards: it only just righted itself as it slipped
back into the sea. Fortunately I had a Bren and two hand-
grenades on board. The shark got two depth-charges and a whole
burst before she ceased to interfere with my dhow's marital virtue.
If anyone is interested in the habits of this fish, my friend Major
Gavin Maxwell has written about it; he made an industry of
hunting baskers with machine-guns and selling shark-flesh (one
of the best meats in the world) to the London market, pure white
flesh, which the Londoners sell in the fried-fish shops as 'rock
salmon'. It is the trade name for shark. There are no rock salmon
anywhere round England. These baskers come close in-shore to
the Berlengas and should be avoided, since their ponderous
caresses are even more awkward and perilous than those of an

[1] Start by buying *Calamares en Su Tinta* in Old Compton Street, London,
W.1.

E

octopus and could be mortal. Of all fish these prehistoric monsters are the toughest to kill. Octopuses, too, are almost impossible to kill with a knife. The only way with a small one is to push its head through its mouth and turn it inside out. With a big one or a squid one has to bite it between the eyes, where there is a vital nerve near the skin.

There is a great deal of archæological exploration, such as Cousteau is doing in the Mediterranean on Sulla's sunken galley and other wrecks, to be done in submarine Portugal. At Troia, situated near Alcácer do Sal, by the mouth of the Rio Sado, there are Roman and Phœnician ruins and the *amphoræ* of a wrecked wine-ship under the water. The best way to get to Troia is by motor-boat from Arrábida or Setúbal across the bay.

This bay is very good for spearing turbot, sole, and other flounders. It is shallow and sandy all round Arrábida, which is a grand rocky hill covered with rosemary, thyme, and stychus-lavender, with a famous monastery on it, and well worth a visit thrown in with one's fishing excursion. There is also a mammoth grotto of a weird, beautiful light and colour at the sea-base of the cliff. It is near Sesimbra, an unspoilt fishing village which is as yet unselfconscious with visitors. The boats are pulled up the beach by hand,[1] and the day's catch, which may include anything from a whale or an oarfish to a sardine, is spread out on the beach every evening. Many weird and rare monsters are to be seen there. The commonest big fish are ribbon-fish called *peixe espada* (swordfish) because they resemble the blades of swords, of which their heads would be the hilts. They are a kind of flattened eel of a silvery-bluish hue, though without scales. They can also give a nasty bite with their fangs. The commonest small fish, of course, are sardines and *carapau*, a baby horse-mackerel which is delicious in August and September.

If you do not like swimming in cold water, you should do your underwater fishing east of Sagres. Except for the big sandy lagoons and estuaries full of mullet, the fishing is more or less

[1] At Nazaré and Figueira da Foz it is done by oxen.

uniform along the whole coast, and does not differ except in abundance from what I described at the Berlengas.

Another poisonous customer to beware of is the delicious sea-scorpion, a hideous red fish with spikes all over him and venomous glands at the base of his spines through which there is a duct like that which grooves a snake's fangs. One should beware of them when feeling about for crayfish and octopuses in the holes in the rocks. This is the *rascasse* that is the chief component of that famous dish, the bouillabaisse. There is also the weever, the English corruption of vibora (or viper) or, in French, *vive*, a small fish which hides in the sand and if trodden on stings with a spine on its head. The fishermen believe that the pain ceases on the ebb of the tide, irrespective of when it was inflicted.[1]

In the old days there used to be three Italian three-masters which came along this coast before Christmas-time to get eels. Their holds were converted into eel-tanks: they coasted Portugal for morays, which were kept for them in floating baskets, and then they went to the two richest eel districts in Europe—Valencia and the mouth of the Rhône. It was on one of these boats, the *Santa Maria, inside the eel-tank,* that I had the queerest underwater adventure in my life and was bitten by a moray, a Portuguese one, though it was an expatriate one. We stopped, on the way home to Genoa, Ostia, and Naples, at Martigues, where the eels are saved up in *vicriers* for months, like electrified piles of macaroni, bounced in nets on the weighing-machines, paid for, and shot wriggling and slithering into the hold. The mate, Signor Moro, slipped in the eel-slime and vanished into the mass of eels in the hold. Three of us went after him with ropes round our middles. We came up to breathe now and then, but it took us a long time to find him, and when we did he was too dead to respond to artificial respiration. It was then I got a nasty bite, but there was a chemist's shop near the quay of the canal, where we

---

[1] The local doctor at Sesimbra confirms this. My friend, the poet Rob Lyle, parallels this with the fact that a peach stain cannot be washed out till the peach trees are in bloom and that the fermentation of wine in bottles, however far removed, coincides with that of the original vineyard.

were anchored. Within three minutes I incised the bite and applied permanganate of potash, which is the only remedy (besides serum) for blood-venom, though too slow for nerve-venom. I record this incident though it did not happen in Portugal, but under the water, and it contains a tip for anyone who is bitten or pricked by morays, weevers, *rascasses*, or ribbon-fish—namely permanganate, which is also a remedy for scorpion, tarantula, and centipede venom, the only chemical remedy known outside of animal serum. If you camp out among the rocks on the Berlengas it is wise to be provided with it, since there are scorpions and centipedes on land there.

The recent Franco-Portuguese submarine explorations, carried out in the abysmal depth, or gulf, which sheers down just off Sesimbra, have given the most interesting results. The bathysphere made twenty-one descents, in all, to a depth of 2,200 metres, a little over 7,000 feet. The two Portuguese warships *Faial* and *Terceira* acted as bases for the operations, carried out by Professor Peres of the Faculty of Marseilles, aided by Dr. Ruivo of the Institute of Marine Biology of Lisbon, who published the results in the *Diario* of Lisbon.

These discoveries are of the utmost importance in view of the increasing soil erosion of the earth's land surface, which, combined with the vertiginous increase in world population, poses a serious question about the future nourishment of the human race, and indicates the sea as our chief hope. Contrary to the experiments hitherto carried out in the deeper parts of the Mediterranean, it was found that, instead of decreasing with the depth, the supply of plankton increases the deeper one goes down in the Atlantic, and reaches its maximum density at the very bottom of the gulf. Contrary also to the case in the Mediterranean, not only does the plankton increase in density, but the fish and polyps increase in quantity. The scientists saw millions of *actiniæ* and *penatulæ* (semi-transparent, flower-like polyps). In the depth off Setúbal they were visited on the bottom by many weird monsters, amongst which Dr. Ruivo mentions, notably, the *halosaurus* with a long undulating tail, the *haloporphyrus* with long antennæ on its back, tiger-marked sharks, rays which lovingly embraced the bathysphere, brotulids, stomiatids, and shoals of big-sea perches. They saw forests of sponges, coral, and madrepores. The deep sea bottom was perforated, like a sieve, with the holes of some unseen molluscs and from the sediment grew beautiful single-branched corals: in fact it partly resembled the ordinary shallow underseas that we are so familiar with, but never become accustomed to, because of their limitless fascination. All the fish at those great depths, says Dr. Ruivo, appeared to be stone-blind, since they showed no reaction to the flashing of light for the first time in that perpetual night of darkness. What was strangest of all was that at those depths powerful currents were encountered.

It is a curious thing in nature, that those animals which eat the smallest mites of plankton become the hugest, and those which live on the largest animals become the smallest. The great blue whale of the Indian Ocean, to which the vastest dinosaurs of pre-history are mere flyweights, and the sperm-whales of Herman Melville mere featherweights, live on nothing but 'krill': and it used to be a terrific sight from the Durban whalers to see them devouring lanes of blue water through the solid red floating masses of tiny crustaceans, which we call krill. Let us hope that, when we human beings have to take to a similar diet of plankton, that it does not swell our proportions to the size of blue whales, so that we crowd each other off the edges of the continents. Yet in spite of the havoc wrought amongst the smaller animalculæ by whales, baskers, and the like, it would seem that the small fry more than get their revenge. What other animals are so bad-tempered as a black rhino or a wild elephant? And it is all due to their being devoured, day and night, by millions of tiny gimlet-snouted, tweezer-beaked, pincer-jawed ticks, fleas, and other tiny parasites. Even whales, the greatest persecutors of animalculæ, suffer occasionally from barnacles—especially right whales, which are so sluggish that anything from mussels to barnacles can take root on them. But the blue whale (with a cruising speed of thirty knots!) very seldom lets anything interfere with his streamlining, unless the *Edda* or the *Odd* of Durban happens to be around, or a Portuguese hand-harpooner.

It is only in Portuguese waters that whales are still fished *by hand*, regularly, with the hand-harpoon, especially in the Azores. This is quite worth a trip over to the islands to see. The biggest thing that the Yankee whalers (even at the height of their fame) would tackle was a sixteen-knot sperm whale. Melville dismisses the 'sulphur bottom', or blue whale, as a giant beyond the powers of man to hunt: but the Portuguese hunt both the blue whale *and* finner—the swiftest of all! The Azores are as good for underwater fishing as the Berlengas; if they are not quite so rich in crayfish and lobsters, they are richer in spearable fish. Dentex especially and *garopas* (groupers) grow to a great size there. There are two layers of dentex: the twenty-five to thirty-pounders are under fifty feet. The water is not so cold in the Azores as it is in Portugal, north of the Tagus: you can swim for longer and you will find a greater percentage of the populace interested and helpful in your fishing there than on the mainland. (That is saying a lot!)

It was hoped recently to restock the northern rivers with salmon, but I understand on the best authority that one cannot expect results for some years yet. However, there is excellent freshwater fishing in many of the smaller streams, especially up in the serras, where some of the streams are so unfished that the trout will come and nip your feet while you are swimming. In the Rio Cavado, between Amarante and Vila Real, I began to feel like the 'Pobble who had no Toes' in Edward Lear's poem. Many of these highland streams and rivers are swarming with trout; and as for the Izaak Walton sort of fishing, the smaller rivers are full of carp, chubb, eels, frogs, and mud-tortoises. The eels are delicious and can be caught even by tying a line to one's finger and then going to sleep by the waterside, or reading a book. My farm is on the small River of Maçãs (Apples), and even as I write here at my desk on the balcony, I have been beckoned three times from my seat by the wagging of my rod, clamped under a stone, to land a fine long silvery eel.

CHAPTER FIVE

Portuguese Horsemen
and Horses

EARLY ROCK-DRAWINGS found in Eastern Spain show that
horses were thoroughly domesticated in the Iberian Peninsula
in the Neolithic age, long before they were tamed in other parts of
the world. We see from Assyrian and Egyptian friezes that they
were early in the field with chariots and cavalry, but when the
Iberians first appeared in civilized Europe, their more advanced
horsemanship revolutionized cavalry tactics. It is known that
horses were being ridden as cavalry, and that a form of light
jousting on horseback, like the modern *escaramuca da gineta*,
existed in Portugal as early as the Neolithic age. Anti-cavalry
weapons, such as the halberd and the calthrop, have been unearthed dating from those times, both in Portugal and Spain. The
calthrop is an unmistakable missile with three points, one of
which always remains bolt upright as soon as it hits the ground,
so as to pierce the tender 'frogs' in the middle of the hooves of
horses: they were thrown in front of advancing cavalry to cause
disorder. Javelins, such as are used today in the bullring, and
weight-balanced lances for one-armed use on horseback, date
from the Bronze Age; prehistoric horse-bits and spurs have been
unearthed chiefly in that part of Portugal, the Ribatejo, which is
devoted to raising horses today. Stirrups, of course, were invented centuries later. But the oldest bits and spurs are unearthed
in Portugal and Spain.

Xenophon is generally credited with being the 'father of
modern horsemanship', but even that great authority, in his
Peloponnesian War, hands the priority to the Iberians, as being

more advanced, for he tells us that Dionysius, the tyrant of Syracuse, brought fifty Iberian horsemen from Sicily to Greece, in 400 B.C., who flung the Greek armies into disarray, by repeatedly emerging in loose order from their own army, discharging their own lighter darts from a longer range than the Greeks were able to do, and galloping back unharmed to their own ranks. The Greeks were already mounted, but fought in another manner. These tactics of discharging missiles from out of range, which appeared so original then, have since been adopted throughout the ages by cavalry as different as that of the Parthians, that of Cortes, that of the Redskins of Sitting Bull, and that of the Boers, of whom tiny handfuls could wear down huge armies of tens of thousands of Zulus and Matabeles, by riding out of range to reload, and then returning to the onslaught. Xenophon tells us that the Greeks had to learn, from the Iberians, these tactics of skirmishing and hurling light darts from long range, before they could hold their own with the army of Dionysius.

The Romans later widely used the Iberian form of warfare and enlisted thousands of Iberian mercenaries. We get our word skirmish (*escaramuça*) from the Portuguese, and it is very likely indeed that these first Iberians to be seen in action outside Iberia were *campinos* from the Ribatejo, seeing that that part of the peninsula is the most anciently horse-conscious, just as the peninsula is the most anciently horse-conscious region in the whole world. Besides, the horse fair at Golegã (with that of the Saintes Maries and that of Beaucaire) is the most celebrated and ancient in the world: and it takes place on the banks of the Tagus or Ribatejo. That some of these fairs date back to Phœnician, pre-Roman times, can be seen in some of the dolls, sold for instance at a place like Janus, a few miles from where I live, where they sell pottery statues of the old Phœnician goddess Astarte, or Ashtaroth, with her wasp-waist, upheld bosoms, and the snakes winding around her, exactly as in ancient Tyre and Sidon. There can be no mistaking her identity. Some of the fairs seem to date back to even more primitive cults of worship—for instance, the one at Amarante, where cakes are sold in the unmistakable shape of a phallus, and given openly by the young men to the girls they are courting, without apparently raising any blushes or bash- fulness, being such a long-standing custom.

At all these fairs the gipsies are much in evidence. They are real wizards at passing off rickety old Rozinantes as good horses, and go to the most fantastic extremes of *maquignonage* in order to get away with clever frauds. But if they know the person to whom they are selling a horse, and, what's more important, if *he* knows *them*, they play fewer tricks. One trick is to deprive a hat- rack of an old horse of water, and let him have a good lick of salt, mixing it with his fodder, too, so that the next day he will drink till his stomach is just one big balloon of water, filling out all the wrinkles and corrugations in his hide and diluting his digestive juices. Then his mouth is opened, and his head held upright, while a live eel is slid head-first down his gullet so as to tickle him up inside his stomach and make him prance about. The oldest crock of a horse, thus treated, will come along frisking and skip- ping about like a two-year-old, for at least long enough to get him sold. They also resort to gaseous as well as aqueous inflation and tamping of the horses. The deflation is sometimes so violent as to be audible and visible. When it occurs the culprits are generally at a safe distance from their indignant victim. I was telling that great horseman, my late dear friend, Aimé Felix Tschiffely, about this eel trick, when he went to his bookshelf and produced an ancient eighteenth-century horse-coper's manual in English, which he had just picked up at the Edgware market for fourpence, and he showed me where he had found exactly the same eel-trick described in detail, in the peculiar jargon of the horse-copers of the time, and rendered the more quaint by the antiquated print with *esses* like *effs*. So it has long been a part of the horse-dealer's repertoire, and was never confined to one country.

The words *escaramuça da gineta*—skirmishing on horseback— are used in speaking of the modern Portuguese jousting, which has recently been revived and popularized by a prominent agro- nomical engineer, Dr. José Rosa Rodrigues, himself a well- known equestrian bullfighter, after a lapse of three centuries. It

differs from the heavy-horsed jousting of northern lands in that
the armour, shield, and lances are much lighter, the lances are
manipulated by hand, not by arm-and-hand, and the joust is not
fought in a closed field, but in the open. Each rider's left side is
covered with a small buckler. He wears a helmet and a light coat
of mail, and bears a light balanced lance, a sabre, and a dagger. It
is one of the prettiest sights imaginable, as the adversaries wear all
the pageantry of mediæval heraldry and repeat all the heraldic
formalities with trumpets, challenges, flags, and caparisons. The
horses are light and sure-footed. There is nothing phoney or
Walter Scott-ish about the costumes. From a practical point of
view, they were evolved for the purpose: nothing 'contemporary'
would be more fitting. The riders manœuvre round each other in
circles as though sparring for an opening, like fighting cocks, and
charging when the adversary is off position. Points are scored by
moving round one's adversary's horse in such a manner as to
strike him on the side unguarded by his buckler. The lance is so
light, and so balanced in weight, that it is manipulated with one
hand, and is never 'couched'. Sometimes up to a dozen performers
skirmish simultaneously, and this, on a smooth green field, with
the dazzling colours and costumes of the protagonists, makes a
beautiful sight.

The Moors learned the *escaramuça* from the Portuguese, and it
became their favourite way of skirmishing between their opposed
armies. The Moors at first were not keen horsemen, as they were
to become: they first entered the peninsula on foot, learning to
ride and fight on horseback from the foes they vanquished.
From 711 to 1500 this type of light-jousting was continually
practised between Christians and Moors, and the latter became as
mad about bullfighting as their enemies. It is wrong to say, as
Quevedo does: '*Jineta y canas son contagion moro*' ('Horsemanship and bull-spearing are a Moorish contagion'). From the
escaramuça the whole science, technique, and art of mounted bullfighting, so unique a feature of Portuguese horsemanship, eventually evolved, as did also that ornamental type of riding which is
known as the *Haute École*, which was taken from Portugal, by the

Spaniards, to the courts of Paris, Vienna, Budapest, and Berlin. The eighteenth-century (Federica) costume, however, is worn when the Portuguese are bull-fighting or practising the *Haute École*: the mediæval rig is only used for the *escaramuça* because of its absolute fitness for it. I have heard theorists put forward the very reasonable thesis that the *Haute École* is the result of teaching the big heavy northern horses of Flanders, brought by Charles V and Philip II, to imitate the nimble lightness and neatness of the horses used in the *escaramuça*. It became a form of sport, a game of skill, and a feat for emulation. An equestrian bullfighter, when he rides in on the first ceremonial parade to pay his compliments to the president of the bullfight, often rides a sort of Verocchio horse, which he could never use in a bullfight, but which he puts through the nimble capers of a smaller horse, making it keep time and waltz to the band; and then take two or three jumps on its hind legs before getting into its natural position on all fours. In fact this is done in most bullfights, and in Spain, where they are allowed to kill, Portuguese riders often jump their horses, upright, over the dead bull.

The priority of Portugal and Spain in all things relating to equestrianism is reflected in the vocabularies of all horsemen throughout the world, even when the spelling is changed almost beyond recognition. The equestrian Boers of South Africa use the word 'kraal' to signify a stable or enclosure. It is even used for a native village enclosed in a stockade. It is simply the Dutch way of spelling the word corral as slurred on the first syllable by the Portuguese. They also owe the finest cavalry marching song in the world to the fact that a Portuguese joined the Boer army and had a song made up about him by one of those anonymous minstrels, both poet and composer, which the 'equestrian nation' produces so prolifically wherever it survives: from the singing *campinos* of the Tagus to the *digters* of South Africa, like Visser and Celliers; from the singing cowboys of North America, to the balladists of Australia, and the '*payadores*' of the Gauchos on the pampas, who have produced the greatest literature of the lot, and the finest music. This Portuguese who gave us our South African marching song went by the name of Ferreira, which is commoner in Portugal than Smith is in England, and *means* Smith, or, more literally, Farrier, just as Herrera means Smith in Spanish. That the English were not very far behind the Portuguese and Spanish in things equestrian is attested by the commonness of the name Smith in England too, showing what a big proportion of the population must have been originally employed in the honourable and useful occupation of shoeing horses. It seems very appropriate that a Portuguese 'Mr. Smith', the descendant, probably, of some army farrier who would be the likeliest first to merit the surname, should be responsible for giving an equestrian nation like the Boers such a rattling good cavalry march as *Vat jou goet en trek Ferreira*. But throughout the world outside of Asia the equestrian peoples derive not only songs but most of the vocabulary, and the instruments, used in relation to their trade, from the Portuguese or Spanish—whether it be the cattlemen of Canada, or the boundary riders of Australia. Words like corral, rodeo, lasso, buckaroo, stirrup, martingale, caracole, roan, bay, colorado, pinto, palomino, etc., etc., all Iberian derivatives, are everywhere used in equestrian countries; and this alone would attest the priority and pre-eminence of the Iberians in all things equestrian, for, as we are told, 'In the beginning was the Word', and it would appear, in this respect, that those who got in the first word also have the last word.

The two first prose-works ever written in Portuguese had much to say about the management of horses. John I (1365–1433) of Portugal wrote the first prose work in Portuguese, about hunting, which naturally had many wise instructions about the breeding and management of horse and hound. But it was King Dom Duarte (1392–1414) who wrote the first of many charming books on how to ride, that figure as landmarks in early Portuguese literature. It is partly from King Duarte's book *Learning How to Ride Well* that Dr. José Rosa Rodrigues began to think of resurrecting the *escaramuça da gineta* so faithfully.

In 1670 Dom Antonio Luís Ribero, a gentleman equerry of the Royal House of Portugal, published in Lisbon the *Mirror of the Horseman in both Kinds of Seats*—meaning both with the long and the short stirrup then going out of use. This book has excellent 'tips', even though it devotes itself exclusively to the mere 'sports' of horsemanship, for I consider bullfighting on horseback to be a *sport* compared with bullfighting on foot, which is a *vocation*, like the military profession or the priesthood, especially as most *toreros*, like all professional soldiers or priests, are morally superior to other men: and I would take as my examples Belmonte, Lalanda, Ortega, Litri, Manolete, and Dominguin. Ribero's book deals with four 'sportive' ways of riding: that is to say *canas*, or bull-spearing; *sortija*, or tilting at the ring; *torear*, or bullfighting proper, and *Carrera de Gala con capa*, showy horsemanship with a cape—the predecessor of *Alta Escola*, or what we call *Haute École*.

There is already a sort of glib 'refinement' and decadence in the attitude of Ribero and some of his contemporaries, in their books on the art of riding. *Adornos*, or acts of prowess, had previously been dedicated as gallantries to women. Now is was simply 'art for art's sake'. One contemporary of Ribero's, Davila y Heredia, referring to the gallantries and chivalries of old times, says: 'Love is blind; but what is *really* required is that the toreador should go straight for the bull with his eyes open.' Another much more famous book than Ribero's came out the same year, in 1670. It was written in Portuguese by Captain Francisco Pinto Pacheco, and was entitled *Tratado da Cavalaria da Gineta*, and dedicated to his most Serene Highness, the Prince Dom Pedro of Portugal. This book carries, as a subtitle, the following words: *com a doctrina dos melhores authores* (with the teachings of the best authors), and it is a compendium of erudition, in which the author draws as much on his wide reading as upon his equally vast experience. This book refers to cavalry drill and operations, and serious, practical horsemanship, although there is the inevitable chapter on bullfighting, with this amusing sidelight on the fights of the time. *Those who enter the bullring with masks on their faces evade their responsibilities and obligations, because this manner of entering the arena gives one far more licence, and allows one not to*

*observe all the rules strictly, if one is so base as to wish to profit by
such licence.* This book gives tips on how to fall comfortably, or
how to lose one's hat or lance without losing one's dignity in
front of the ladies.

The most important and compendious of all the books on
horsemanship written in the Portuguese or Spanish languages is
the *Arte de Cavalaria da Ginete e Estardiota, bom Primor de
Ferrar et Albeitaria* [1] by Antonio Galvam d'Andrade. In a launda-
tory sonnet by which the volume is prefaced, the poet, Dom
Antonio Alvares da Cunha, says the author is 'unique both in
theory and practice': and the author himself thoroughly endorses
this opinion in a self-laudatory prologue, emphatically (though
truthfully) enumerating his hippic accomplishments and abilities,
for which he had been distinguished from the age of seven. He
was sixty-seven when he published this book in 1678. His advice
presupposes that the reader is already an expert both in the bull-
ring and on the field of battle. But he is a refreshing, dynamic,
lovable, and generous personality, all the more so, in that though
he insists rigorously on keeping the technical rules and regula-
tions, he is even more of a stickler for courtesy, ceremony, good
nature, chivalry and gallantry to ladies, which makes him seem
quite old fashioned when one compares him with his less human,
more 'modernistic' contemporaries, who reckoned that love produced poor tilters and toreadors, 'being blind'. This masterpiece
of Galvam is divided into three parts: the first devoted to the
breaking in and riding of horses, their exercise, and all the feats of
skill that can be performed by riders on horseback; the second
part referring to *estardiota*, or mounting horses with the modern
bit and bridle with long stirrups, dealt with what was still then
something of a novelty imported from Italy; the third part dealing
with veterinary work, shoeing, and harness.

It will be remembered that Ribero's title for his book mentions
'both types of seat' and that Galvam devotes a whole second
section of his book to *estardiota*. The two seats co-existed for

[1] The Art of Riding on Horseback and the Use of the Bridle (Estardiota),
and the Good Mastery of Shoeing and Veterinary Medicine.

some time till the short stirrup with the calves, bent backwards almost at right angles, began to be displaced by the long stirrup with calves almost perpendicular, about the end of the sixteenth century, 100 years after the Moors were finally driven out of Spain at the fall of Granada in 1492. This new way of riding was not generally and popularly accepted till later. The revolution it performed was to transpose the steering from the knees, aided by a weak bit, to a strong bit. Before, at least half, if not more, of the guidance of the horse was done by kicks in the belly and the pressure of the knees, and very little by the bit, though in primitive riding, before the invention of the stirrup, the seat of the horseman resembled the modern seat, with calves hanging perpendicular. The first stirrups to be invented, and used for many centuries, were therefore short stirrups. These short stirrups were taken by the Moors to Africa,[1] where they are still preferred to long stirrups: and, personally (having seen both styles in action), I am not sure which is the most effective. What you gain with the one style you lose with the other. For quick short-range manœuvring I feel sure that the old style is more effective. Cavalry is out of date, though a sudden old-fashioned cavalry charge has been twice successfully performed in the last twenty years. A charge of heavy cavalry was the only thing that managed to delay the German advance into Warsaw for twelve hours, so stunning was the shock: and I was privileged to see the mediæval Iberian cavalry style, exported from Portugal in the fourteenth century, when the Lister Division and Andre Marty's 13th International Brigade (mostly Senegalese) were breaking, and the Moorish cavalry went into Brunete after them with lances on 25th July 1937. The rapidity of their evolutions and the dexterity with which (with one hand) they wielded those light lances, as they cleared around and over the tombstones of the cemetery, where the Reds were making a desperate resistance, was an eye-opener to me. For I had thought the Moorish lancers more to resemble horseguards on parade in full kit; I had thought they were rather

[1] This style of riding can still be seen at State functions in Madrid when Franco's Moorish Guard follows the coaches of Ambassadors.

for ornament than what they proved that day. One infantryman, in my hearing, said of the 6th Tabor of Melilla that day, that they *'salieron como unas exhalaciones'* (they shot out like meteors, or fiery exhalations). I never heard a finer description of *anything*.[1] This lot were riding on the short stirrup, using knee guidance, with streaming pennons, cloaks and turbans of brilliant colours; and imagining the even brighter colours and waving plumes of the Portuguese Christians, I can see why the poets of the golden age both in Portugal and Spain, anonymous and known, were so fond of comparing armies and battles to gardens and fields of flowers: and again comparing flowering gardens and meadows to regiments, armies, and the nodding of the coloured plumes on the heads of the horses and the helmets of the knights. We have a fine example in English copied by Patmore from Tirso, where he compares the blaze of dandelions and buttercups to

> The six-thousand-voiced shout
> Of Jacob camped in Midian put to rout.

Then there is that fine, flowery image of a knight falling from his horse which exists both in Spanish and Portuguese, and could be Englished thus:

> A noble cavalier came riding
> So swift a horse, he left behind
> And seemed far swifter than the wind,
> For in his speed, the earth deriding,
> With feathers streaming in the air
> That, with their meteor plumes aflare,
> Made him a phœnix to my view—
> He did not touch the ground, but flew,
> And gave such colours to the air
> As if the Springtime with the sun
> Disputed, alternating, there

[1] Reversing the comparison of the Spanish soldier, the great Portuguese-Moorish poet Sara of Santarem (who died in A.D. 1009), in a poem on a meteor, compares it to a charging cavalryman. My army-Arabic is both shaky and rusty, but here is my effort to translate it. "The shooting star seemed like a lancer when the swiftness of his charge unravels his turban and trails it streaming after him."

(One with her coloured blooms and one
With starry beams)—which was more fair.
His jewelled ostrich plumes took wing
Mingling their sparkles in such showers
That now he seemed the Solar King
And then was Flora, Queen of Flowers.
He raced, he fell, and then lay still
So that which seemed a bird before
Seemed like a giant rose to spill
Wide open on the grassy floor.
Who ever saw it might suppose,
United in one single creature,
Stars, wind, and sun, bird, beast, and meteor,
All culminating in a rose.

This is no doubt exaggerated, but right up till the Boer War, soldiers competed in the majesty of their appearance by the beauty of their uniforms. Some of Napier's eye-witness descriptions of battles, as late as the Peninsular War, take on the beauty of gorgeous, movable colour schemes. And no writer of prose, not even Melville himself, can evoke more vividly ineffaceable isolated figures, as when he describes the first Portuguese grenadier to get on the walls of Ciudad Rodrigo charging the French army alone and disappearing into thin air in the red blaze of the explosion. I often wonder if the *Flowers of the Forest*, when the English had butchered all the wounded at Culloden, was suggested by the coloured plaids and kilts lying on the battle-field.

We can see from such paintings as Uccello's that mediæval battles were even more brilliant from the point of view of flowery colour, just as they were apparently more chivalrous and humane (even when waged with Moors) than battles at later dates.

In these drab days, when we are forced to wear such mousey colours as a sign of general slavery, it is good to gaze on the few splashes of bright colour which have survived in male attire from better ages—the uniforms of the Life Guards, the costumes of *toreros* and *rejoneadores*, and even the spangles of acrobats and

F

costers. In Portugal there are still the regional dresses of the people (strictly non-utility) and there are many smart cavalry regiments, and, above all, the ancient surplices with all the splendour of church regalia and ritual.

In the torrents of literature written about horsemanship in the seventeenth century, horseworthy readers may have noticed the vast amount of space devoted to *enfrenamiento*, the use of the rein and the bit, or what the Portuguese call *estardiota*. Galvam devotes a third of his book to it. Nowadays most of the questions have long been settled. We have arrived after centuries of experiment not only at discovering the snaffles, curbs, and bits which exert the greatest braking power with the least strain to horse or rider, and finding out the gentlest bits for the tenderest mouths: we have also rediscovered and unearthed the strong bits used before the invention of the short stirrup. So what has been settled and become obvious to us is taken for granted. Galvam may seem long-winded in spite of his very great charm. Yet it is to riders and writers like him that we owe the puzzling out, step by step, of what is now common knowledge.

It was, however, while reading two other books, *Theory of Gineta Exercises* by Bernardo de Vargas Machuca, and the *Discourses* of Dom Donivan Arias Davila Puertocarrere, second Count of Punenrostro, being the Jinete of the greatest Grace and Beauty of his age, in 1590, that Dom José Rosa Rodriguez really was able to reconstruct (thoroughly) the old joust and put it into practice as we see it today, an achievement of outstanding grace, skill, and beauty. The other kind of heavy jousting we tried out in France first on horseback, but it was too expensive: and then on fast motor-boats, when we stepped up the old nautical jousts of Provence, till we exceeded the speed of the old carthorse-chargers, but it was too costly in life and limb, especially, but not only, because of getting chewed up in the propellers: and the law stepped in, in 1931, to revert it to its old form as a survival of the old Roman *naumachia* (the *joutes nautiques*), on rowing-boats or slow motor-boats doing under five knots. The chief casualties (apart from propellers) were caused by the heavy shock of the lance on the plastron; even when deadened, as always, with cushions, it caused pulmonary lesions: and I often wonder if this does not account for the early mysterious deaths of good heavy jousters like Gaston de Foix, the Black Prince, Henry V, etc. Apart from straightforward, visible injuries the Portuguese *escaramuca* does not implant hidden lurking deaths like the lesions that carried off five of my confrères in *La Joyeuse Lance Martégale*; still, I believe, the champion team of the reformed, reduced, and softened jousts of Provence.

Nothing, if you can find really safe stabling for your horse, mule, or donkey, is more pleasurable than falling in with the long straggling processions of mingled riders, muleteers, donkey-drivers, cyclists, carts, carriages, caravans, cars, and pedestrians on their way to horsefairs at Golega, Santarem, Silves, Evora, and other country places. Here you will see a man and his wife pedalling laboriously fore and aft of what seems to be a tintinnabulating pagoda, but is in reality a miniature Woolworth's stall on six wheels, sandwiched between a bicycle tandem, with a pistol-firing monkey sitting before the male partner with his tail round the bow handle-bars. As he navigates through the crowds he bumps with his front wheel gently into the hind quarters of Capitolina, the she-goat (who dances on her hind legs, upright, on the tops of bottles). Her owner, who has her on a lead, leaps from his donkey to the ground and inspects the behind of the goat for damage. There is a loud altercation, encouraged cheerfully on all sides by the admiring crowd. The monkey, whom the sight of the goat enrages, joins in the altercation, in paroxysms of gibbering fury, to the huge delight of everyone. The goat, nose in the air, regards the monkey with stony contempt. Meanwhile the better stern-half of the tandem dismounts, joins in, and tells the goat-expert what to do with Capitolina. Finding the odds against him, the goat expert retires with his goat and donkey, telling the fore-and-aft tandem couple what to do with their monkey. As this excites the loudest laughter of all, he repeats the sally and seems to be adjudged the winner, for he remounts his donkey with his chest expanded, and the goat, still nose in air,

steps haughtily along beside him. There is a sudden tintinnabu-
lation of saucers, cups, egg-whisks, looking-glasses, pots, and
pans, as the shimmering hardware pagoda begins to weave its
way, navigating more gingerly this time through the crowd.
Here you will find blind guitarists, lame accordionists, Punch-
and-Judy showmen carrying their outfits on their heads, with all
the hawkers of peanuts, knife-grinders, chestnut roasters, sunflower seeders, and sardine toasters, trundling, head-carrying, or
pedalling their various contraptions, ovens, grills, and charcoal-
stoves to the scene of action.

You will also see handsome *campinos*, in their full regalia, with
green-and-white stocking caps, red waistcoats, white silk sleeves,
and long white stockings, with shouldered lances, carrying their
wives and sweethearts, in their Sunday best, a-pillion behind
them—a common practice in all horse-countries, from the
Argentine to the Camargue. When you come to the scene of the
fair you will see splendidly dressed ladies, beautiful amazons,
landowners, and horse-breeders, in *torera* jackets (like Eton
jackets) with silver-grey sombreros, and cavalry officers in
uniform, jostling with mountebanks, showmen, and graceful
gipsy girls with long dresses, like Indian women's, reaching in
folds to the ground. Every kind of horse will be on show:
Percherons, cavalry horses, hunters, beautiful huge show horses
for parades, and Alta Escola, race-horses, jumpers, and everything else, from a Clydesdale to a Shetland.

In dealing in horses, as a mere *chalan* and horsebreaker, *without
any capital*, I have had more than thirty years experience of the
gipsy people without ever trying to fraternize with them or to
copy their habits, as my more wealthy friends have been able to
do without losing caste; such as Walter Starkie, Augustus John,
and others who have done so, greatly to the profit of Art and
Literature. My dealings with them have been those of a hard-up
competitor engaged in the same struggle for life. It has often
come to knife-wounds and blows. As I infinitely preferred the
French, Spanish, and Portuguese peasants to most of the gipsies I
have met; as one cannot be friends with both lots, without being

a rich man; and as till lately, I always grew my own bread and wine, by the sweat of my brow, I naturally prefer those who work, like I do, to those who, however charming and picturesque they may be, live better by flattering rich travellers, hikers, tourists, and the like, than by their own hard work in the adopted countries they live in, as I do.

But I made my peace with them in the Spanish War when they were hunted down wholesale by the Reds (as they were in Russia and Red Hungary) and all the chalans, horse-copers, minor toreros, and farm workers had to throw in their lot together against the wealthier 'intellectuals', factory workers, miners, liftmen, bootblacks, waiters, and menials, whose bosses threatened to collectivize and enslave all non-union workers, as the peasants and gipsies were finally subjected in Russia by starving millions of them to death, though they stuck out to the last. It did not help to belong to the Vaquero's Union as I did—farm workers were despised as kaffirs. When I first started breaking in horses I was nicknamed *emplasto*, or 'sticking plaster', throughout the lower grades of the horse trade from Toledo to the Algarve, and even when I was at daggers drawn with the gipsies, they only tried to cheat me twice because they have a natural respect for a good rider, and they always addressed me by the name that I earned chiefly from being trained to ride from early childhood on calves and steers with wobbly skins—hence 'sticking-plaster', though, later, after a fight I had with the Bargas tribe or clan on the Roman bridge of the Alberche river, I was re-christened *Tres Manos* or 'Triple Hand'. I was completely reconciled to the Bargases during the Red Terror, though I still bear the scar of a Bargas knife wound on my neck. The Bargases have shifted to Barcelona now, and their place has been taken by the Lozoyas, who have always been staunch friends of mine, through thick and thin, at Toledo, Santarem, and at San Pedro market, where they still deal in horses—one mile from where I live.

In my chapter on the fado I have recounted (where it is more apropos) how the gipsies succeeded in cheating me with a deaf mule to my eternal shame as a *chalan*: here I may recount how at Silves in the Algarve they tried to cheat me, before they knew me, with a mare that proved a bargain, since I bought her for a song, 200 pesetas, or two pounds (as it was then), though I would have given twenty pounds for her straight off—if I had had the sum. Her original name was Demonia, or 'she-devil', but they rechristened her Garota, or 'dear little girlie-wirlie', in order to get rid of her quick, and give the impression that this man-killer was as sweet-tempered and innocent as she looked. Actually she had already killed two men and the last victim, whom she had savaged with her teeth by the scruff of his neck, was in hospital in Portimão. I believe, if I hadn't bought her, those gipsies would have paid me 200 escudos to take her away. The police, in Portimão, had gone to have her destroyed, but the gipsies told them they had already shot her, sawn off her hoofs for glue (they had some glue to show the police made from a recently dead horse), towed her out to sea with a big stone tied to her neck (which they carried in the boat), and then when they had sailed into the deep water off Carvoeiro they had dropped the stone overboard and sunk the dead horse for the sharks. Only one fisherman lives at Carvoeiro, and they had given him a much-coveted charm to ensure good catches of fish: this magic 'medi-cine', which, once a net has been anointed with it, is supposed to confer wonderful catching powers, is known as *mermaid's fat*. The sample they gave him was a dud—mere pig's grease, or may-be the fat of the horse whose feet they had recently glued. But nevertheless he swore to, and did, back the gipsies' tale. The real article should be accompanied by at least a square inch of the skin of the *sireia*, siren, or mermaid, to prove it is genuine, but a piece of porpoise-hide does just as well. The fisherman was easily pleased.

A genuine trade is done in the fat of this rather disgusting, but extremely human, animal, the manatee—of which you can some-times see a highly pornographic specimen on show (as a 'mer-maid') at Olympia. I last saw it at a fair at New Orleans. I can always recognize it by the chip in its left flipper. It has been round the world several times and is rather the worse for wear. The first time I saw it was at a fair in Paris, in 1918, with T. W. Earp (who gave the English language the word *twirp*, really *twearp*, because of the Goering-like wrath he kindled in the hearts of the rugger-playing stalwarts at Oxford, when he was president of the Union, by being the last, most charming, and wittiest of the 'decadents'), Nina Hamnett (the 'Laughing Torso'), the beloved Marie Beerbohm (Max's niece), her cousin, the utterly beautiful Iris Tree, and Beatrice Hastings, the South African circus rider beloved of Modigliani. The same stuffed 'mermaid' was still functioning last year at a fair in Louisiana as the rival of 'the Egress'. 'Come and see the EGRESS: only a dime!' You went into an empty tent with an open egress through which two enormous all-in wrestlers firmly but politely 'bounced' you out of the back of the tent!

I came across mermaids on the Rufigi River while trading in poached rhino-horns when supposed to be coast-watching as a sergeant in the last war: the Arab who bought my rhino horns which are finally sold in powder as aphrodisiacs to Chinamen on the other side of the world was quite a character.[1] This Arab came to me and said: 'You shooting one Goddam bitch, what stay in river called merdmaid: me giving you 100 shillings every time.

---

[1] Since writing this chapter, the veteran rhino-hunter, Senhor Faria, my neighbour at Sintra, informed me that the Chinese are right in their belief that rhino horn is an aphrodisiac, and convinced me with the following dissertation. 'The so-called "*horn*" is not made of horn but of *hair*. It is a coagulated, solidified, and concentrated BUN of hairs, which the Almighty, in a jocular and satirical mood, placed in the inverse position to the nape where buns are generally worn (that is partly why rhinos are always so furious.)' Then, pointing to my bald head, he continued thus: 'If hair were not an aphrodisiac, why did our all-wise Creator place it so copiously on the heads of the most beautiful women, like banners to wave us on to the onslaught. You who have translated the two finest '*hair-poems*' ever written, Quevedo's *On Lisi's Ginger Hair* (see Chapter Two) and Baudelaire's *Chevelure* should be ashamed of your ignorance! Why also did the Divine Creator, Who made us in His image, dispose hair on the amatory parts of our bodies and keep it there long after the hair of our heads has departed (as in your case) to leave a skating-rink for flies? If mere tufts of it can serve as ensigns and incentives to love, think of what a solid chunk of it, weighing

I want fat and skin. I leave you meat. . . .' I had heard of these
animals, for whom the natives have a vice, to which the 'mermaids'
yield with pleasure: just as the Lacandon Indians of Brazil have a
vice for making love to alligators, which gives them the disgusting
disease pinto, like leprosy. Their feet turn white and fall off. It
was therefore that I knew the fisherman had been 'done down'
when he gave evidence later, because every piece of mermaid fat
should go with a piece of skin and it is of a pinkish quality. He
showed a sample of pure white lard or dripping. I asked the
Arab what he did with the fat. 'Me selling to man in Mozambique.
Make plenty good *dawa* (medicine). Portugal man catching fish.
That man sending fat to Portugal. Plenty money. You shooting
hittamus-tottamus too. Native man making dawa. Me pay big.'
He suggested I use an amorous native as a decoy or stalking horse
for shooting 'mermaids'. The best way to get them to come out
of the water was to sit on the wreck of the *Königsberg* and play the
ukulele.[1]

I do not apologize for this diversion, since the trade in charms
and medicines is intimately connected with the horse-trade, and
in Portugal every lower walk of life is dominated by witchcraft,
which still exists in parts of England too in quite a big way. A
book could be written on witchcraft in Portugal. For what reason
I do not know (as I am not an initiate), but the talisman most
sought after by horse-dealing gipsies is the real head of the
amphisbæna or two-headed snake—the 'blindworm', whose head

---

from forty to fifty pounds, can do to a full-blooded Chinese Mandarin, who
is already amorously inclined, and has few moral scruples.' I now agree with
my friend, who reminded me of all the glorious poems written, and pictures
painted of hair. But I would sooner be kissing the red-gold fire of Lisi than
the rhino-horn that nearly got me in Mozambique last year. The Chinese
can have all the solid hair they want. I like mine fibrous. But I believe they
powder the so-called 'horn', and mix it with snuff, or introduce it surreptitiously into the tea or swallows'-nest soup of their intended victims. For
other jokes played by the Almighty on rhinos see p. 41 of my *Light on a Dark
Horse*, where I give the other reasons why rhinos are always so furious.

[1] The *Königsberg* was a German raider in World War I. Her wreck, which
was bombed by my brother, lies in the Rufigi river.

so resembles his tail as to be almost indistinguishable. I saw one of these put up to auction by a mountebank last Sunday at San Pedro fair, and it did not change hands till the last bidder plumped for a *conto* (1,000 escudos—£12 10s.). Well, when I bought Demonia, the she-devil (alias Garota, or sweet little girl), the gipsies, to show me how sweet-tempered she was, shouted '*Abaixo*' ('Down'), and the beautiful mare, arching her neck, immediately lowered her back for me to mount by stretching out her forelegs and her hind legs to an angle of about forty-five degrees. I was delighted at this trick. I had brought my wife a-pillion to Silves on a pretty gelding called Garoto (by a strange coincidence), in other words, 'dear little chap', a name he merited in every way: a black Arab with a white face, who seemed to be the twin brother of Demonia. They were as like as two sardines. As I had no spare bridle I leaped on to her bare back and took the rope of her headstall, not knowing the danger I was in, though the bargain price of her should have warned me that all was not well. Algarve horses are as pretty and dainty as sable antelopes. My wife on Garoto, and I on Garota, hit that lovely turf road, a horseman's heaven, that runs, or ran in 1936, from Silves to Estombar, where I was spending sick leave from the Madrid front. After such horror and carnage, to be riding in peace with the person one loves more than the world, and looking back over the valley at Silves, one of the most beautiful of all towns (except that peer-less queen of beauty and valour, Toledo), I was in the seventh heaven of delight. Bee-eaters turned green and gold in the dying shadows on the red earth when they swooped near the ground. Rounding the corner, we suddenly came upon one of those ambulating pedlars of tin and china chamber-pots who, in the days when they were an innovation, used to trundle from farm-house to farmhouse, singing their praises, and all but demonstrat-ing their practicality. We call those pedlars of ewers 'smousers' in South Africa, and when I was introduced to the late Sir Abe Bailey *as a poet*, the delightful old gentleman proudly smote his chest, and said, 'Damn me if I didn't start life as a poet too!' He then told me that he had begun life as a PO-et, a 'smouser' hawking PO-etry round the Transvaal, and explaining the convenience to Boer women of not having to go out on the veld of a frosty night.

At first sight we were dazed by what appeared to be two mountains of white cuckoo-spit, each of whose bubbles magnified a million times to the proportion of these magical ewers, ornamentally patterned with cerulian twirls and twiddles. On approaching nearer, we saw it was two mules each carrying a tremendous pile of these ornamental novelties, as they were then. In the midst of the leading pile, the only sign of a human proprietor, bobbed the upright tassel of a stocking cap, giving a piratical, rakish air to the whole outfit. Garota had sailed into a beautiful, voluptuous, racing, rippling run, as smooth as velvet, which she could keep up for miles and was quite as comfortable as a trippel or a canter, even without stirrups. Other horses had to go at almost a hand gallop to keep up with her run. She reminded me and others of Seton-Thompson's story *The Pacing Mustang*. I used to run her on the chalky soundless path on the top of the cliffs near the English resort of Praia da Rocha, just to listen to the exclamations of delight and wonder which the English people (the least phlegmatic on earth), mistaking me for a native, because of my clothes and sheepskin chaps, would vociferate as I went by sitting back like a Spaniard and bolt upright, without a single tremor of movement or undulation from her long level stride, which was almost soundless, like black velvet. When we approached, both the mules, carrying about 1000 chamber-pots between them, began to rise off the ground as if the earth were red-hot, like springboks 'pronking', with all four feet at once, arching their backs and precipitating first of all the Galician,[1] who rose up against the sky like the mannequin tossed in a blanket in

---

[1] The Galician smouser, Senor X, was not ruined by Demonia's second demolition of his stock-in-trade. He later swept the whole of Portugal, Spain, and France by patenting the highly popular device of having an eye painted looking upwards from the bottom of these utensils, which struck people's sense of humour and sent the sales rocketing so high that he retired after two years and now owns a big hotel in Vigo.

Goya's picture, with his head on one side, standing bolt upright in the air, then fell to the ground amid showers of his own hard-ware and crockery, which detached themselves in resounding salvoes, clanking, rattling, and spilling into so many fragments that an American archæologist, ten years later, when the frag-ments had all been trampled in, though he had discovered a whole mass of ancient Roman pottery and the remains of a large tessellated floor, with mosaics and all! He tried to sell them to the Museum at Cincinnati, city of blessed memory! It was only when, after infinite pains, with the aid of plaster of Paris, they *restored* one of these 'urns' from the mass of splinters available, that the somewhat prosaic nature of the archæologist's discovery became apparent. The fragments were eventually deposited (after coming all the way from Portugal to the junction of the Ohio and Mississippi) on one of those glass mountains which are beginning to rival the Rockies and the Sierras Nevadas in the American landscape, simply because in the U.S.A. it is less labour and expense to manufacture a new bottle than to rinse an old one. At the rate North Americans drink, these twinkling, glassy sierras are threatening to assume Himalayan proportions and already cover hundreds of square miles! The two mules went on bucking, till not only the last of the ewers had sailed away, but a girth split, and one of the saddles was catapulted into the sky, and took quite a long time to come down.

By this time the smouser had the head of one of the mules and I had the other, having passed Demonia's headstall rope to my wife. Far from tranquillized, the two mules were still vociferating a sort of rumbling wheeze of protest. Drawing a deep breath, the Galician Po-et extended his hand to anathematize the mare (whom he apparently recognised) in prophetic words which I will translate thus: 'Accursed be the tripes of the mare that bore you: accursed be the genitals of the stallion that begot you, you foul she-devil and murderous, mad mare!' Then, turning to me, he courteously lifted his tasselled stocking and continued: 'Sir, what sort of a man are you who ride that murdering she-devil bareback on a headstall?' 'Señor, you must be mistaken,' I said;

'I have never ridden a tamer horse.' I said '*Abaixo*' to the mare
and she complied, looking like a lamb, with the sweet hypocrisy
of Tirso's *Maria la Piadosa* from whom Molière copied his
Tartuffe, just as he copied his Don Juan from Tirso's infinitely
superior original. The Po-et said, '*I* might be mistaken. But how
could my mules be? They knew her at once and smelt her even
before you came in sight. She was drinking at the same trough
with these two mules in Lagos the other day, when she suddenly
went haywire and kicked them both sideways with the same
damage to my pots as you witness today. She even bent some of
the special hardware ones, which were guaranteed unbreakable
and were made in a far-away country, called Birmingham' (which
he pronounced Beer Ming Ham with the accent on the last
syllable). My wife and I tied our horses to an olive tree and began
to help him sort out the tin pots from the broken crockery. We
both expressed grievous concern and sympathy for the loss of his
stock-in-trade. But he reassured us that he had always had his
wares insured for double their value, and that apart from the discomfort of being deposited on the ground, he had suffered no
damage on either occasion when he had met with *that*! Here
he cocked a snook at Demonia, Garota, or whatever you like to
call her. Again I said it must be mistaken identity.

I was so worried about what he told me about my new-bought
mare, that I rode back to Silves with Senor X, the vendor of
private, ornamental conveniences. My wife rode home alone.
The gipsies, to whom I brought the police, when accused, swore
that this was a different mare from one which they lyingly said
they had destroyed three weeks before, naming the fisherman at
Carvoeiro, whom they had dishonestly bribed with bogus mermaid's fat to bear witness. I went to see the fisherman, and he
swore blind to having deposited a dead horse in the deeps. On
the showing of the mare's exemplary conduct, I believed the
gipsies and the fisherman. I gave up the idea that she was a killer,
on her own showing. She behaved so well that my little daughter
Anna, aged ten, was riding her bareback. But a strange fatality
occurred. At this time I went back to the front for three months,

and being wounded with a bullet clean through my shoulder-blade, and a broken collar-bone, I had the good luck to be allowed to come home to my wife. Meanwhile this mare had endeared herself to the whole family and all the neighbours. Then came Saint George's Day!

Saint George used to be the Tutelary Saint of England till he was demoted in favour of Saint Oscar Wilde, by the Society for the Prevention of Cruelty to Dragons, because this outrageous Christian, Saint George, the patron saint of picadors, caused unnecessary suffering to an anthropophagous dragon, by depriving it of its daily breakfast in the shape of a beautiful virgin princess, and giving it a 'pic' just where all cannibal dragons should get it—that is to say 'in the neck'. But Saint George is still revered in Portugal.

Then occurred the strangest fatality ever seen by me, and it seemed to be in keeping with the allegedly fatal reputation of Garota as a killer.

As she was the handsomest horse for miles around, she had the honour of carrying the statue of Saint George in the religious procession. The statue carries a light spear in his right hand. In this procession we gild the hooves of the horses (about thirty or forty) with gold paint, weave flowers and ribbons in their manes and tails, and take the saint for a little joy-ride round the village of Lagoa, singing hymns and stopping at a few of the taverns. The sacristan insisted on leading Garota and holding the right leg of Saint George so as to keep him in the saddle. I was holding the other leg. It was just then that one of those lovely big gusts, that blow off the Atlantic, opened fire and filled everyone with joy and ozone. Just above our heads was a magnificent buxom young matron standing on a balcony, to the *right*, to watch the procession. We both tried to keep from star-gazing up her skirts, but this almighty blast opened her frock with the elating crack of a parachute filling; it was like the hoisting of a great rosy spinnaker! —but instead of masts, we saw a pair of legs that were more majestic than the mainmast of the *Victory*. That frock started to slat like a sail in a hurricane: then it ended up by tying itself round her neck, unwinding again and ballooning itself to the skies over her head. Neither the sacristan nor I could help looking and beholding the live statue of Ceres herself! The whole village nearly fell on its back with delight and admiration, and there were resounding cheers while the blushing lady fled to her inner apartments. Neither the sacristan nor I could help letting go of Saint George's legs, so thunderstruck were we with admiration for this wonderful sight. It was just then that Saint George plunged and struck: the spear went clean into the sacristan's heart. He did not even have time to let out a cry. What a wonderful clean death— at the hands of a saint! And in sight of the Rose of all the Winds. If you ask them in Lagoa why they no longer take Saint George for his annual pub-crawl, that is why. This sounds a tall story. But the priest, the mayor, the local doctor, and anyone else will tell you the same. If only the upside-down lady-parachutist had been standing on the balcony to the *left*, nobody could have been killed—Saint George (he is a hefty piece of work) would have lurched leftwards. He would have knocked me over, but the spear would have been harmless. For, at that moment, you could have knocked me down with a feather! But you can still see Saint George and his fatal spear in the church at Lagoa.

It was about this time that the fisherman from Carvoeiro had the gipsies up. Since he had used their mermaid fat he hadn't even caught a blenny, let alone a carapan or a sardine! He reckoned this 'fat' was not only useless, but baleful. I only had to attend the case for ten minutes. I could have told him what fat it was if I had got nearer to it. But to this day I could not tell anyone what the case was about!

Now this is where I come to the most extraordinary thing about Garota. I had ceased to believe in the smouser's story of her being a killer (which was true). I happened to put on very big spurs to deal with a big horse at Portimão, who had thrown everyone else that tried him. His name was Hitler, and he was also a bad lot, for he eventually injured his mistress permanently. My shoulder was still open, but the bone was setting. I rode Garota to Portimão, to the rendezvous near where they had the big horse that I was to break. I was absent-mindedly dismounting from Garota in the central square when she (whom I had not touched with the spurs) went absolutely haywire, squealing like a hundred wild boars, and going off like a packet of crackers on the fifth of November. She had waited till I had one foot on the ground and one in the stirrup. Then, curving her neck to bite, and alternately rearing and kicking her heels to the sky, she went round in circles. I had not the strength to pull myself back in the saddle because of my wounded shoulder, though my hand was gripping the pommel. This lasted a minute. When she gave up (though with bad grace), trembling all over, there were about twenty English tourists from two autobuses taking photos of us. If anyone remembers this, I would be grateful for a snap of that tussle—the worst I ever had with a horse. If she had got me on the ground I should have been dead with two hind kicks in the belly.

The police raised a row about this, but as everyone, including the horse, was scatheless, they could do nothing. Yet someone told them it was a condemned horse that had been surreptitiously rescued. I saw there might be a bit of trouble: so I thought of reporting back for duty at the Legion H.Q. at Badajoz. My papers were all in order. She was behaving like a lamb again. I swam her across the Guadiana by night and sold her to one of the best breakers I know in Merida, Señor Muñoz. He sold her to Monasterio's cavalry.[1] Four years later I picked her out in a fair at Talavera and bought her again. By that time she was a quiet, good horse. We even inspanned her into a carriage, which we borrowed for a picnic; the Señorita Josefina Bosch y Damm of Barcelona, daughter of the Brewers, my two daughters, and my wife, all hefty people, and all good horsemen, though we knew nought of carriage-driving, jumped into the cart, with the result that the shafts went upright and Garota was suspended in the air on a steep incline, where all five of us started on a proper death ride towards a cliff. It was my wife who saved us by heroically

---

[1] Rather, I should say Mounted Infantry.

throwing herself on to the back of the horse and restoring the balance just before the acceleration of the cart had become irresistible, and would have dragged the horse completely from her foothold.

We sold her back in Lagoa when I came over to volunteer for the English army in 1939. A tamer horse you never saw than she *became*. But if you are buying horses in Portugal, buy them in the Ribatejo: *not* in the Algarve, where they breed those dainty black demons. Though Garota became a good girl and may today be carrying Saint George again, in heaven, she was a typical black Algarve horse, involved in three deaths and two attempted murders.

Nobody visiting Portugal in the next few years should miss the sight of that supremely great horseman João Alves Branco Núncio before he retires (for he is now fifty-six). This man is a blue-blooded aristocrat with a pedigree reaching back centuries. Handsome, kind, gentle, modest, and beloved by everybody, it is he who, by the lightness, grace, and gentleness of his style, seems to lift his horses, while they dance the *Haute École*, or as they weave round bulls, as if his stirrups were the winged sandals of Perseus and he had the great wings of Pegasus grafted into his shoulder-blades. I have never seen such beauty, grace, skill, and good breeding in the actions of any man. If you see him riding you will not wonder why the word *caballero* means gentleman, or why the word chivalry came from this wonderful prehistoric relationship of men with these noble but rather simple animals, for a horse has nothing like the brains of a bull or a cow, and only about a third of the intellect of a donkey or a zebra. Morally, I would say the same of that great Spanish *rejoneador*, Alvaro Domecq, of Jerez de la Frontera, the founder of schools and hospitals, but nobody else has that balance of dash, style, and grace of Dom João Alves. There are at least twenty other good professionals in this peninsula worthy to rank with our immortal Pat Smythe and Colonel Llewellyn. I saw the Portuguese Francisco Mascarenhas kill a bull from horseback in Madrid when he was ten or eleven, in 1939. He is still all dash and fire, and he can plant two short banderillas from the saddle as befits the scion of so many conquistadores. But the fact remains that it was Dom João who first planted a both-handed pair of banderillas from the saddle, and he is the only man to have estocaded a bull from the saddle since the Indian Ceballos, depicted in his prodigious stunts in Goya's etchings.

CHAPTER SIX

Gado Bravo and the Campinos

THE WORDS *gado bravo*, meaning wild livestock, are a slurring of the Spanish words *ganado bravo*. *Ganado* is the past participle of *ganar*—to gain, to win, or to earn: but it becomes a noun, just as the present participles 'earnings' and 'winnings' become nouns. To put it in a nutshell, it means WILD WEALTH. For *bravo* means either 'brave' or 'wild', or both at once. It could hardly mean brave as applied to a rabbit or a pigeon. Similarly Isla Brava and Costa Brava mean Wild Island and Wild Coast. Applied to the wild species of European cattle, the word means both brave and wild, in a superlative degree! The idea of wealth originated in cattle. The Saxon word sterling, with its diminutive ending, refers to a small steer, as duckling refers to a small duck: and the original pound sterling was a token representing the value of a steer. Similarly our word pecuniary comes from the word *pecus*— meaning a beast. Our word capital, meaning money, came from the word *caput*, meaning head, and refers to head of cattle. The word stock originally referred to livestock on a stock-farm. But with all human beings the unreal symbol eventually supplants the reality for which it originally stood. And so the unfightable, inedible, indigestible, unyokable, unmilkable pound-note became the object of human acquisition in the place of the valuable, beautiful, and useful animal it represented. That is how the inedible, unfightable golden calf supplanted the real one, and in spite of the divine prophet Moses, who smashed it up, we have gone on scrambling for the pieces ever since.

'Wild wealth' could be used to describe the fisheries, the whaling industry, the fur-trade, the herding of reindeers, the poaching of rhino-horns to sell for aphrodisiacs to the Chinese, the poaching of ivory, filming wild animals, or selling them to zoos, and as all these activities determine the way of life of those engaged in them, so does the highly specialized work of the herders and graziers of fighting cattle determine their way of living, their psychology, their customs, superstitions, and traditions. But first let us describe the country where they live.

A towering scarlet, white, or orange sail, lit up transparently by the sun, seems to be travelling overland, like a disembodied flame, as it rustles through olive-groves, over ricefields and cornfields, to disappear over the horizon of low pasture-land dotted with cattle and horses. Then a second sail flutters, in a different direction, along another of the low-lying invisible canals, watercourses, or tributaries of the Tagus, which criss-cross the swamps and plains of the Ribatejo (or Tagus bank). Before it reaches Lisbon and debouches into the Atlantic through a very narrow outlet for such a big river, the Tagus forms a large lake, at the opposite end of which is Vila Franca de Xira, and the first bridge over the river, a magnificent piece of engineering. Vila Franca is the capital of the cattlemen, as Golegã, farther inland, is the capital of the horsemen.

On the wide grasslands the white silhouettes of beautiful horses (a domestic breed) and of the great wild fighting bulls stand out against a background of wind-blown clouds, coloured sails, skies of an intense azure, so blue as to be almost black, fringed on the horizon with the grey-silver of olive-groves, the blue of eucalyptus, and the dark green of umbrella pines. In Portugal the winds are always at work, and do much of the transport and water-pumping, besides grinding the corn and pressing the oil. When the sails of the boats cannot be seen, then it is the sails of windmills, and beyond them the tireless eternal acrobatics of the clouds as they swirl in their silver contortions on a heliotrope sky. Rob Lyle, who has shared all my travels in Portugal, has called his forthcoming book on Portugal *Rose of the Winds*—the most perfect description of this country that was ever given.

The country known as the Ribatejo, and that to the south of it,

known as the Alentejo (Alem Tejo: Beyond the Tagus [1]), is the
territory where the *campinos* lead their wild, fantastic lives. They
are to Portugal what the *gardiens* are to Provence, the *vaqueros* to
Spain, the *vaccari* and *buffalari* to Italy, what the boundary
riders are to Australia, the *gauchos* to the Argentine, and what the
cowboys and buckaroos (*vaqueros*) were to the Wild West before
they deserted the saddle for motor-cars.

The minute you get into Vila Franca you will be sure to see
several of them lounging about in their curious costumes. Most
of the cattlemen of the world conform to the Spanish model in all
things, including dress, with a wide hat and chinstrap, a short
torera, and a pair of goatskin or sheepskin chaps over the trousers,
which are of the kind known in the army as 'drainpipes', spurs
with big rowels, and high-heeled boots. The Spanish do not keep
wool on their chaps, but decorate the tanned leather with intri-
cate patterns in poker-work. The chaps and saddles of the
Spaniards are amongst the most beautiful leather-work I have
seen. The disadvantage in taking off the fleece of the chaps is that
you are not so warm in the winter. The Portuguese keep the
wool on so that you can use the chaps to keep warm in winter,
even if you are only sitting up writing late at night, without a
fireplace, as I am doing now. I always wear my Spanish chaps in
the summer to show off with, and my black *caracul* Portuguese
ones in the winter. I am wearing the latter now not only for
warmth but because with the wild, freezing north-easter whinny-
ing and crashing through the pines outside, they make me feel as
if I was astride a horse, and that the horse is Pegasus himself.

Apart from the chaps, the costume of the *campino* is completely
different from that of any other kind of cattle-man. He wears a
green stocking cap with a golden tassel and headband, a scarlet,
sleeveless felt jacket like a waistcoat, through which the full
sleeves of a white silk shirt are thrust to button at the wrist. The
campinos never wear their sleeves rolled up. From the waist down
they wear black velvet knee-breeches with thick white stockings,

[1] Perhaps the best translation, on the analogy of Transvaal or Transkei
would be Transtagus.

gartered at the knee. A line of silver buttons runs like a guards-man's trouser-stripe from waist to knee. As Sacheverell Sitwell says, they have something almost 'Neapolitan' about them. They have ornamental saddle-cloths, and their handwoven striped blankets are works of art.

Just as the cattle-men of every country evolve their own music —from the cowboys of Western America to the *gardiens* of Provence, the *gauchos* of South America, and the *vaqueros* of Andalusia with their *cante jondo* or flamenco songs—so the *campinos* have their special way of singing their melancholy *fados*, a kind of song which is as unique in music as is the *cante jondo*, with the same kind of '*miaulement*' that, in poetry, we only get in Baudelaire and, in music, in a few of the Highland and Hebridean laments. All cattle-men use the guitar. Except the Portuguese, no nation of cattle-men anywhere in the world fails to follow the Spanish lead in its dress, favourite musical instru-ment, and in its vocabulary. The Portuguese cowboys are an exception to the universal acceptance of the Spanish lead in all things taurine, vaccine, and bovine, but only in their way of dressing, both inside and outside the bullring.[1] The Portuguese *rejoneadores* dress *à la Frederick* when they are fighting bulls on horseback—that is to say, in the costume of the time of Frederick the Great. They wear three-cornered hats, patent-leather boots reaching to the thigh, and embroidered coats of green, red, orange, or yellow silk, with coloured ostrich plumes in their hats.

As in Pamplona, one of the taurine capitals of Spain, and the Saintes Maries, the taurine capital of France, on festal occasions bulls are loosed in the streets, and the young men race with them through the town of Vila Franca, to the accompaniment of fire-crackers, petards, rockets, and ear-splitting yells as casualties are tossed head over heels in the air. Fatalities are quite common.

When you cross the bridge at Vila Franca de Xira you pass the *campinos'* church, whence on the festal occasions of rodeos,

[1] The costume of the Spanish *rejoneador* is exactly the same for a ceremonial bullfight as for riding to cattle—working kit.

bullfights, or stampedes the priest blesses the cattle to keep them healthy, wild, and, above all, fierce and brave, without which qualities this particular species would have become extinct and been supplanted by domestic breeds. Around this church the plains are dotted with herds of bulls, cows, and calves. On the opposite side of the road, a little farther on, is a hotel-restaurant with a small bullring. This restaurant is called the Gado Bravo, or Wild Cattle Hotel. Here, some days every month, when there is a bull in the arena, if you become bored between the courses of this hotel's very excellent cuisine, you can jump over the barricades and torry the bull with your table-napkin, and a very effective lure it makes too, since a bull is far more sensitive to a white than to a red rag. In the old times the *muleta* or sword-cloth always used to be white, but for modern bullfighting it overexcites the bull: modern fighting capes are magenta inside and yellow outside, not because yellow or magenta attracts the bull more than any other colour, since bulls, like most mammals, are colour blind and see white better than any other colour, but simply because they look pretty. There is only one unarguable axiom about the vision of a bull; it is this: that, irrespective of colour, a wild bull will always make for the nearest moving thing, however trivial, and will lose interest in any object or shape, however big, as long as it is motionless.

The life of the *campinos* is conditioned by the nature of the cattle they exploit. One must remember that they are wild animals just like the seal-herd of the Pribiloff Islands, which are none the less wild animals for being protected, sorted out, escorted on their annual migrations, and occasionally thinned out for their fur, by the United States Navy. Otherwise one might compare them to the wandering herds of caribou or reindeer which are none the less wild for being followed and exploited by Eskimos and Lapps.

The management of the bull both inside and outside the arena is dictated by the reflexes, the psychology, and the physiology of the species. It even dictates the way of living of the cattle-men. Wherever this species exists you will find that identical customs

have been evolved independently in parts of the world as completely isolated from one another as the Camargue in France, the
Campagna in Italy, and the Ribatejo in Portugal, which is cut off
from the cattle country of Spain by the acorn-and-swine country
of Spanish Estremadura. Except for the use of the lance in
preference to that of the bolas or the lazo, which are invaluable for
cattle such as Herefords and Longhorns, which try to get away,
but no use on cattle that charge and thereby slacken the rope,
cattle-men, whether herders of domestic or wild cattle, throughout the world conform in almost everything: in their preference
for the guitar as an instrument of music, and for the knife, rather
than the effeminate and clumsy fisticuff, or the inartistic mechanical revolver, as a settler of accounts; in their use of the horse as
an ally; in their strict code of honour and monogamy [1]; in their
dances; in their arrogance, boastfulness, pugnacity, and hardi-
ness; in their use of the box- or bucket-stirrup to protect the feet
from horns; in the wearing of leather chaps; in the homogeneity
throughout the world of the *vaquero* saddle, which enables you to
sleep on horseback; in the habit of loosing bulls in the street on
festive occasions, and in many other things besides.

To explain the way of life of the *campinos* we must first of all
study the character of Bos Taurus Ibericus, as this species is
baptised by zoologists, though it once inhabited the whole of
Europe. Sub-species of it can be found in places as far apart as
England and the Cape of Good Hope. It is of a similar strain to
the fighting cattle of ancient Crete and Egypt. The last auroch
to be killed in Europe outside Spain was killed with a musket in
Poland in the early years of the eighteenth century. A portrait of
it can be seen in Domingo Ortega's and the philosopher, José
Ortega y Gasset's, joint booklet, *El Arte del Toro*, of which I am
the proud, fond, and fortunate possessor of a copy inscribed to
me, jointly, by the greatest *torero* of his age and the greatest
philosopher. This auroch is simply a Spanish bull, without any
difference except the lighter colouring, which seems to grow

[1] Here the *gauchos* of the Argentine can be excepted—to 'prove the rule'.

lighter as one gets farther north, as is the case with foxes and hares. The survivors of the almost extinct Chillingham herd in England are similar to the bulls of the Ribatejo in physique: it is only in their pale cream colour that there is any variation, and also in the manner in which they used to be coursed or hunted, well into the nineteenth century. The 'sportsmen' used to sit in the branches of trees with fire-arms and shoot them as they were driven by beaters through the woods. No wonder the Anglo-Saxon does not like real bullfights! Here is a curious anomaly: though it is difficult and dangerous to drive a single animal, a herd will always run before a single person. Hundreds of buffalo, too, will flee from a single person or a single lion, yet it requires more than one lion to deal with a single full-grown buffalo. A solitary bull or buffalo is almost invariably dangerous.

Bos Taurus Ibericus is the fiercest and bravest of all wild animals. There are two domesticated sub-species descended from it: the breed of Herens in Switzerland, and that of the Afrikander [1] in South Africa. In both these latter cases domestication has modified the aggressive angle of the horns, but it has not yet removed the powerful tossing muscle which rises like a triumphal arch between the horns and the shoulders of the un-castrated males, and is the distinguishing mark between wild and tame cattle. This muscle can be seen on an even grander scale on the neck of the gigantic Bos Taurus Cafer, or African buffalo, though when we tried these beasts out in the Portuguese bull-ring at Laurenço Marques, and in the native bull-rings (a survival from the days of the Portuguese *conquistadores*) on Pemba Island, where bullfights persist even under British rule—they disappointed us, and proved far less exciting than they are in the bush, where many experienced hunters consider them to be more ferocious, tenacious, cunning, fierce, and dangerous than grizzlies, leopards, lions, tigers, elephants, or rhinos. But in the arena they

---

[1] The word Afrikander is often applied by Englishmen to the human inhabitants of South Africa, who are Afrikaners without the 'd'. Afrikander, when applied to a human being, is an insult for it carries the secondary meaning of cuckold.

were far less dangerous than they are in the bush: and far less lively than the smaller, quick-turning bulls of Portugal and Spain, for, after charging once or twice, they jumped the barricades, which conduct on the part of Bos Taurus Ibericus would be accounted a disgrace. In nearly all the experimental duels staged between Bos Ibericus and elephants, lions, tigers, and bears, the bull has won; though Martial records a rhino killing a bull; and in 1634, on the occasion of the Infanta's birthday, the Portuguese Duke of Braganza provided a tremendous lion which killed the bull. This Duke had a knack of finding tough beasts by way of birthday presents, for when he was sending the Pope a rhino on the occasion of his birthday, it stove open the side of the ship in which it was being carried, sunk the ship, and drowned itself with most of the crew.

The Iberian bull differs from all the other charging animals such as rhinos in that it charges repeatedly, turning in its own length to do so, whereas a lion or a white rhino tends to charge straight on, and a black rhino seldom charges more than twice. I have never been charged by an African buffalo without provocation and only once by a water-buffalo in the Pontine marshes: but I cannot count the times I have been charged by bulls, cows, and even calves while riding on the Portuguese pastures, and on the Camargue. Only last year at Hlu-Hluwe I found myself confronted by a solitary buffalo which had been fighting and expelled from the herd, for there was blood on his muzzle and shoulder. Instead of charging, he shambled off. In the case of Portuguese cattle, such an outcast would most certainly have raised his head and tail, and charged at once. The only thing that disarms such a beast is immobility: which proves that they must be colour-blind, reacting to movement rather than shape or hue. There is a trick known as Don Tancred or 'playing statues', which is often performed in the arena. A man, generally in white, stands completely motionless on a barrel: the bull, ready to charge, comes right up to him but does not touch him as long as he does not move.

In mammals, I often think that the seeing of colours, so distinct to birds, fish, and insects, is partly a matter of education. The more civilized a person is, the more colours he can see. To the raw Zulu grey and yellow are one colour (*mpofu*): blue and green are one colour (*buklazi*): and red and brown are one colour (*bomva*). Considering the luminous beauty of the eyes of cattle ('ox-eyed' being a Homeric title to beauty), it is disappointing to reflect how little they can see.

My neighbour, the Marqueza de Cadaval, was confronted by one of her own bulls on her ranch at Mugem. It had just been slung out of the herd. It was too near (and too late) to lie down and get comfortable, as do the men and women in the ricefields whenever a solitary bull hoves in sight. She stood there for three hours: and every time she tried to move slowly and imperceptibly into a more comfortable position, up went the terrible head and the tail and she had to freeze once more. Bulls do not put their heads down till they are almost touching their target: nor do they close their eyes, as far as I can see, since they follow the cape exactly.

Even castration does not induce the docility in this strain of cattle that it induces in all other animals, including human beings. Once while driving in a car in the Alentejo we experienced the most determined and vicious charge from a domesticated bell-ox, or *cabestro*, of this breed. It was in 1937, at night, before the road to Lagos from Setúbal was metalled: and we were going along slowly in the thick dust which we raised, which a following wind carried before us, and which seemed a wall of fog, scarcely penetrable by the headlight. We heard cattle-bells, and Dr. Pinto, the Municipal Health Officer of Lagoa, in the Alquarro, stopped the car, since, from the sound, a big herd was crossing ahead of us, and he wished to give them time to cross. Suddenly we heard the clanging of one of the bells quite near us, and out of the fog broke a huge horned head followed by a great black body. There was a terrific crash and clang, as he hit the radiator. He withdrew a yard or two, paused, and charged again. This time he must have hurt himself, for he withdrew, shaking his head from side to side, as if stunned momentarily, but otherwise unhurt. He had turned one of the headlights completely upwards so that it shot a vertical beam to what *seemed* an extraordinary height, illumining the clouds which were low over the high plateau. With our combined strength the cowboy (who rode up on hearing the crash), the doctor, and myself (in all some 600 lb. of gristle and brawn) could not bend the twisted iron one millimetre back towards its original position. This was during the Spanish War, when I was back with my family at Lagoa, on leave from the Madrid Front: there had been unofficial air-raid alarms, because the Red Radios were threatening the Portuguese for aiding the Spaniards, as they did in the Peninsular War, to regain their country: but for which self-defensive aid the Iron Curtain might have reached to the Azores.

When we drove through the gas-lit villages, with me in a Spanish uniform, and what seemed a searchlight pointing to the sky, we caused quite a lot of excitement, especially when we had to pass through Lagos itself on our way to Lagoa. The police kept stopping us to ask if an air-raid was expected. So that poor old bell-ox created a tremendous sensation, second only to the fighting bull which escaped from a lorry in the Praça de Pombal in Lisbon last year on its way to the bull-ring: it went on a voyage from the Etoile of Lisbon [1] (which is the Praça de Pombal) to Lisbon's Rue de Rivoli or Bond Street, the Chiado, busting up two tram-cars, heaven knows how many café chairs and tables, and injuring many people. It did not stop till it had twenty-five bullets in it, when it heeled over in the street of the Chiado. I record these two incidents, one concerning a castrated eunuch, to illustrate the ferocity of this species. The two exceptions in human history of brave eunuchs are the cases of Narses and Solomon, the captors of the Vandal King Genseric: Narses and Solomon were worthy successors to Belisarius when he had excited the envy of Justinian and fallen into disgrace. They were exceptions, but even an ox of this fighting species has a lot of fight in him as a rule.

---

[1] London has not got an equivalent—but the distance would be from Regent's Park to Bond Street.

One day, when, to amuse the now-famous authoress of *The Legacy*, Sybille Bedford (who was then only a little girl), I cocksurely jumped into the arena to throw a three-year-old ox and take off its red-and-white rosette for her, I got the surprise of my life. Before I could grab even one horn I was sailing through the air and distinctly remember seeing two aeroplanes from the nearby airport between my shoes! The late Elliot Seabrook, president of the London Group, took a snapshot of this at the apex of my somersault: and I occasionally look at it by way of good counsel, to remind myself always to grab both horns simultaneously and to treat even a yearling with respect.

We must now go on to the organization of the ranches on which these cattle breed. Next to the owner of the ranch, the *mayoral* is the chief manager, who often runs the whole ranch if the owner lives in town, or is often absent.

Next to the *mayoral*, in order of importance, comes the *conhecedor*, the technical expert, or 'knower'. He knows the name, genealogy, character, and appearance of every animal on the ranch, all of whom he can recognize at a glance, as a shepherd can recognize his sheep, unaided by those multiple variations of natural colour and marking which distinguish cattle from one another, even without the infallible aid of branding each with a number and the device or badge of the rancher, with his distinguishing slits in both, or either, of the ears. No two animals are alike in the whole of nature. Though a herd of zebras may appear alike in their markings, which are infinitely less complicated than those of a single thumb-print of the human hand: and though these markings obey absolute restrictions, in that they are lateral on the cheeks and legs and neck, and longitudinal on the spine, shoulders, haunches, and nose—yet no two zebra-skins, when examined closely, even faintly resemble one another. There is no animal in the world whose distinguishing markings differ so widely and fantastically as the bull, or to whose colourings and markings more importance has been attached since the earliest times.

The Egyptians considered their Ox-god, Apis, which was of this species, as the most complete expression of divinity in an animal form, proceeding as he did from Osiris and Phtah jointly. He was chosen from among the millions of Egyptian cattle entirely because of his markings, which conferred divinity. On a black forehead he had to have a white mark in the form of a crescent moon; the figure of a vulture or an eagle had to be seen on his back; and the figure of a scarab in purple or blue on his tongue. So infinite in variety are the markings of cattle that there was always an Apis to be found at a moment's notice, even under those very exacting conditions. After a short time the old Egyptian priests would drown Apis in a fountain consecrated to the sun, when his mummy would become the object of a cult. They would soon find the next one.

In the Portuguese and Spanish newspaper reports of bull-fights, and in all histories of tauromachy, no bull is ever mentioned without reference to his colour and markings (and the shape of his horns, for which there are many expressions), directly after his name, which is given him along with his branded number and noted down on the day of the *tienta*.[1]

The colour is of importance in the breeding of bulls, since though many reddish, yellowish, or grey bulls are very valiant, the over-recurrence of these colours coincides with a falling off of caste and valour in the breed. The *conhecedor* has his memory helped by the variety in the shape and size of horns, the colour and markings in his herd: and it is infallibly reinforced by his notebook with the brand, the name, and the behaviour of the young bull or cow under the stress of branding or the *tienta*. He can be certain of the parentage, since each stud bull with his harem is herded apart by the cowboys, and his cows are listed. The cows stay long enough with, and close enough to, their calves to preclude all errors.

[1] In English we have words like roan, bay, dapple, grey, chestnut, piebald, and skewbald, to describe horses. But the Portuguese and Spanish have at least five times as many adjectives for horses: and as for bulls, their words are so many and so distinct, not only referring to the colour and markings but the behaviour, shape of horns, and ocular expression, that they can present you with the photograph and the unmistakable identity of any bull in four words.

After the *conhecedor* come the *campinos, cabestreros* (those who attend the bell oxen), the grazers and ranch hands, nearly all of whose hobs are inherited from their fathers and grandfathers, and who are all experts at their trades. The mounted *campinos* and grazers are skilled in the use of the *garrocha* or cattle-spear ten feet long, with a point half a centimetre long, or more. The unmounted grazers are known as *pastores* (the same word is used for shepherds of sheep). They are skilled in the use of the sling and the club. They know how to move on foot among bulls with a minimum of peril to themselves, so as not to cut the line of retreat of the animals, always driving them from behind towards other animals if possible, dissuading them by the use of their voices, or their slings even, if they show signs of charging, by erecting their tails. They do not fraternize too closely with the beasts, for fear of making them tame. With their slings they are miraculously accurate, and can strike any beast in whatever portion of the body they choose. The bulls destined for the arena are given the richest grazing and fodder, while the cows and the oxen and calves of under a year old feed on the poorest. Whenever the fighting bulls have eaten their fill on the best, the remaining cattle are allowed to follow them and finish off what is left.

When the young bull or cow is about to be born, the cow finds some secluded and hidden spot in the thick bushes or reeds, where, whether by instinct or instruction, the newborn calf will remain on the spot, where he will die of hunger rather than move to another place, and where he will defend himself against all comers except his mother, as soon as he is an hour old. Even the blandishments of other cows who have lost their calves will not induce him to move in the absence of his mother. The mothers are dangerous if one approaches the calves. Cows speak to their calves and croon to them in tones we can only half hear. The period between conception and birth is nine months, as in the case of human beings, but they grow infinitely faster. A bull of three years old is a respectable adversary in the arena; one of five years a dangerous adversary. The pugnacity and courage of a very small calf removed by force from where his mother has left him and apparently ordered him to 'stay put', while she goes after her own sustenance in order to be able to suckle him, can be appreciated in some of the village games. They kidnap one of these 'stay-put' calves, fix a cocarde to its brow with a thread, then let it into the arena for a 'course libre' of boys under nine or ten. I have never laughed so much in my life as to see this lilliputian course, but one laughs with tears in one's eyes, because the super-comic attitudes of the calf and the boys (who take it even more seriously than does a *toro de muerte* and his executioners, while all of them are in the very valley of the shadow) is balanced by the breath-taking valour on both sides. If the calf sometimes paws the sand—often a sign of weakness or fear in a grown bull—it is only while he rests to get his breath. I have counted twenty small boys all on the ground together sprawling like skittles and nine-pins as one of these calves made lanes through them. After the course, in which some sixty-five children of five to ten years old took part, about half of them needed bandages and plasters. Yet there was only one broken arm.

The cubs of lions, leopards, tigers, and lynxes do not show this impressive heroism that human children and calves show. Children are wonderfully brave, while still innocent. The little children who saw the miracle of Fatima through (all under ten) were told by the 'Progressive' Mayor of their county-town, after being beaten and tortured, and kept each in solitary confinement without food, that if they did not retract their evidence they would all be killed—by being thrown into boiling oil. Each was told that the others had so been killed, but though they believed it and wept bitterly for their little colleagues, they would not retract one word, though they were subjected to Gestapo and N.K.V.D. methods of starvation and mental torture again and again, which they resisted better than grown-up soldiers.

It is no wonder that the two animals who exhibit the greatest valour of all animals (even when they are weak and defenceless) should celebrate their rival valour in a form of ritual, such as the bullfight. Nor is it any wonder that giving proof of such valour in their finest specimens, they should also produce the worst specimens of cowardice too. But it is better to reach supreme heights at the cost of touching the depths, than to live for a mere average, and to subordinate height to an average of security. I have seen the young of almost every animal taken into captivity. A lion cub will forget its mother fairly quickly though it is a noble and faithful animal and will remember a master many years after it has been handed in to a zoo, as too unwieldy a pet. Only a human child, and to a lesser extent the calf of a fighting bull, will remember his mother. Even baby chimpanzees and baby elephants, highly intelligent animals, take at once to their foster-parents, with no regrets.

The lance used by the mounted cattle-men is about ten feet long. It has a sharp point: and is used chiefly for chasing the cattle from behind; but it can stop them from in front, at a pinch. When cattle or buffalo are running, their hindquarters come together high off the ground. The *garrocha* helps one to take advantage of this fact, and of the steady gait of the horse, so that a prod from the *garrocha* as the rump of the bull rises off the ground will easily roll him off his balance. In this way he can be compelled to obey the will of the horseman eventually. Even if the bull charges repeatedly, to be eluded by the speed of the horseman, there will come a moment when the bull tries to get away: and that is the horseman's opportunity. The bull can also be thrown by galloping behind and grabbing his tail, which is swung heavily as one passes him. But this needs practice.

There is an excellent photo of this feat (in the latest edition of the late Aimé Tschiffely's book *Tschiffely's Ride*) of a Mexican general performing it in honour of the great horseman, whose closest friend I had the honour to be. I tried to throw a wildebeeste bull on the Athi plains in this manner during the last war, from a 'Matchless' motor-bike: but I made the unpleasant discovery that although horned like cattle, the blue wildebeeste runs (and kicks!) like a horse. It kicked off the handbrake of the bike.

Other ways of managing cattle, when dismounted, are to get a bull by the tail and the horn, and to revolve with him as he tries to get at one. This is all right as long as one has a friend or two to

Above—The beach at Sagres, from where the first Caravels sailed

Below—The beach at Cascais

Above—Pines in the Serra da Estrela

Below—A Quinta in the Douro

Rob

Casa de Port

take away the bull's attention when one disengages from him. He cannot be thrown this way. He can be thrown only by holding both horns, which is known as *mancornar*; it is an acquired knack of which I am a champion. Buddy Baer's act in *Quo Vadis*, in which he is almost as heavy as the *novillo* with which he wrestles, is the opposite of the real *suerte de mancornar*, in which a small man (by a species of Judo) can overthrow a bull five to seven times his weight. The man who threw the big bull in *Quo Vadis* was a Portuguese *forcado*.

The strongest muscle of any animal is nearly always the easiest to take advantage of in the reflex. Look how fishmongers paralyse the strong claws of lobsters with a piece of flimsy paperelastic to prevent them from opening. A hyena can crack an elephant's bone with the strongest jaws in the world—yet he can be muzzled with a string. The terrible kicking muscle of a horse is rendered powerless when you shoe him just by gently bending back his hoof. The tossing muscle of a bull is terrible on the upward thrust, but he relies entirely on the force of gravity to return his head to its usual position. The slightest disequilibrium throws him over.

Portuguese *forcados* are teams of hefty men, generally six, who form up in a line in front of a bull: the captain takes the charge of the bull's forehead, in his stomach, and gets the horns of the bull under his armpits, with his belly clamped on the bull's horns, and his hands locked at the base. The rest of the scrum surround and subject the bull, while the hindmost man throws the bull by the tail, in the opposite direction from that in which the captain and others are trying to get his horns down. If the bull tries to ram the captain against the barricades, the projecting horns save him from being crushed.

No bull is allowed to be killed in Portuguese arenas, though last year Manuel dos Santos, the matador, killed one on purpose as a test case, and was duly tried, but released because it was the hunting season and *gado bravo* is technically a wild animal. The *forcados* always follow the Portuguese *rejoneadores*, who place banderillas from beautifully trained horses. The bull's horns are

H

padded so as not to hurt the horse, but they are still dangerous: Carnecerito was killed by a padded bull. When the *forcados* have swung the bull to the ground, it is taken away and given the *coup de grâce*, out of sight. However, as soon as a Portuguese *rejoneador* crosses the border (say, to a town like Badajoz,[1] where Portuguese tauromachy influences the mind of the crowd as much as Spanish tauromachy does), he meets the bulls as the Spanish *rejoneadores* do, with naked horns, and he follows the customary three pairs of banderillas, with the *rejon de muerte* or javelin of death, spearing the bull with a vertical downward stroke of the closed fist—not in the lance-couching manner with which a picador receives the charge of the bull.

People of many nations excel in the art of the *rejon*, which, unlike that of the sword and the swordcloth, is not a Spanish monopoly. The great Peruvian horsewoman, the beautiful Conchita Cintron, earned immortal fame as a *rejoneadora*; married to a Portuguese, she now lives in Portugal, and forgetting bulls, thinks only of her babies.[2] Madame Calais, for whom I had the great honour of working as her peon, must have killed some 700 bulls in her time. (Conchita worked in thousands—not hundreds.) She was killed by a stray bullet from the machine-gun of a German 'plane over Paris during the last world war. She was also a very beautiful and good woman, though she got a little stout towards the end. Her famous countrymen, Albert Lescot of the Mas du Village on the Crau, and Pierre Saurel of the Mas Thibert on the Camargue near the Rhône ferry or 'skip', were truly great killers of bulls from horseback—nearly as good as the best Portuguese of whom the non-pareil and supreme artist is João Branco Núncio, who, like some exquisite wine or liqueur, seems to improve with old age. Next to him come the Simão da Veiga, father and son. The father is a painter of talent.

[1] In the old Roman maps, Badajoz and Merida were both included in Lusitania, taking a bite out of Spanish territory of about 1000 square miles.
[2] With typical goodness and charity she came back to the bull-ring (only once) to give a magnificent show in aid of the widow of the matador Carnecerito de Mejico who was recently killed in a Portuguese bull-ring.

The habit of 'staying put', which is probably half inherited and half inculcated by their mothers into the suckling calves, may be that which caused the adult bull, when in peril, to seek to 'park' himself in a *querencia*. The word *querencia* means the 'liking', the preference, or the fancy of the bull. It refers to the spot where, without any apparent reason, the bull, when loosed into the arena, invariably decides to take up his 'general headquarters'. To this spot he will gravitate between the charges he makes against his adversaries. The nearer he is to this spot (his *querencia*), the more confident, dangerous, and difficult to tackle he will prove. He may choose his *querencia* for some strategical advantage—near the body of a dead horse, for instance. But in general he chooses it without any motive apparent to a human eye. It may be in the centre of the arena, or in the middle territory, or near the barricades. The *toreros* are forced to concede him this chosen territory or *querencia* of his, within which he is master and truly redoubtable. The farther he can be lured from it, the easier he is to handle. The area surrounding the *querencia* is called technically 'the territory of the bull'.

To understand the use of the *cabestros* we must take a human parallel. The *cabestros*, or eunuchs, play in the life of fighting cattle exactly the same part as the eunuchs played in the Byzantine Empire—and exactly the same part as the more effeminate 'intellectuals' play in the British Empire of today. Their similar function is that of betrayal of the male principle in the taurine or human community to which they belong. Their respective castration is performed either by compulsory education, generally English public-school, or (after they have been tested in the *tientas*) on the Spanish ranch itself—according to whether they are British human beings or Spanish cattle. At the public school the physical operation would be superfluous. The public school thoroughly tests those whom it does not emasculate, through fear, bullying, sodomy and their own physical masochism, until they become wonderfully tough and brave, but abjectly docile, as far as opinions go: they never think at all: they are given their opinions ready-made and they all hold the same opinions at the same time: then they are allowed to change their opinions (but it must be simultaneously) about ten years after it has ceased to matter whether they do or not. Those who conserve their gender are very brave indeed and will fight to the death, for their collectively induced opinions. People like myself have to be muzzled at the time of such events as Casablanca and Yalta and Potsdam—because the 'authorities' think we are mad. Then they allow some docile personage to 'let the cat out of the bag' about ten or twelve years after it doesn't matter a damn—some tame journalist like Chester Wilmot, who seems to size it all up with a great flourish: but God help anyone who can see what is going on *at the time*! I raised my voice in *Talking Bronco* and my *Collected Poems* in 1945 and '46—but they were 'eliminated' from publicity. Now they are famous books.

The function of the *cabestros* is a parallel to what in Europe has been called the *trahison des clercs* by Julian Benda. A typical example was the betrayal of the brainless, valiant youth of England into the International Brigade by the gun-shy poets of the 'left wing', who had a wonderful time banqueting in the Spanish rearguard and playing table-tennis at posh pensions of the Catalan Riviera. As peace-time belligerents they also trumpeted the youth of England into the last world-shambles which brought them more picnics and vastly remunerative sinecures on the M.O.I., B.B.C., C.O.I., and U.N.E.S.C.O.

The *cabestro* says with his bells, 'Come along with me', then vanishes into a safe corral to chew the hay, while the bull goes into his solitary *chiquiero*, or cell, or pen, to await the hour of battle. We cannot blame the *cabestro* for his character: it is due to the physical operation that has been performed on him, perhaps against his will—on account of his having put up a cowardly show when he was being branded as a yearling, or tested as a two-year-old. He has also his beneficial uses, as when a bull has his life spared by the crowd for nobility and bravery—it is the *cabestro* who leads the bull out to life and freedom. Once the bull was in such a state of fury that he savaged the *cabestro* and killed him. But without the *cabestros* no bull could either be got into the arena to be killed, or out of it after he was pardoned. The *cabestros* and their attendant *campinos*, armed with lances, are sent in to lead out a defeated bull who does not come up to fighting standard. Oftener, the *cabestro* only acts as a Judas to the bull for the sake of the *vaqueros* whom he knows, and loves better, than his own brothers, the bulls. The *cabestros* will often charge any *torero* who is hanging around and who is naturally not known to them personally, when they go in to fetch the condemned bull back to the corral for liquidation. Their loyalty to the herd is that of a sort of Home Guard. They don't go into the front line as commandos for the preservation of their race, as the bulls do, and they must hate the bulls for getting off with the girls: but they will knock over an enemy parachutist if they find him, at a disadvantage. Or, better still, a *cabestro* is a recruiting sergeant who has never been in action.

The power of the *cabestros* over the cows is quite as great as over the bulls, even greater sometimes. It reminds one of those Italian singers who used to get castrated to improve their voices. Their singing had such a hysterial effect on women that it excited them uncontrollably. These eunuchs who had been castrated late in life were not only potent, but utterly tireless in making love, since they never reached the climax. All the famous Italian singers who came to England in the eighteenth century had to flee for their lives from battalions of outraged husbands. I have never seen any amorous goings on between oxen and cows, but the oxen certainly charm them. There are several ways of castration, some by ligature, some by incision, some by amputation—but I won't describe them, since they might suggest ideas to some of our Foreign Office and B.B.C. exoliti. We know that the Roman exoliti used to practise it in order to effeminize their voices.

Cows are liable to develop what the Spanish call 'nymphomaniac' tendencies on very rare occasions. The cow in question tries to mount on the other cows, and the secretions in her vagina become so acid that she cannot conceive from the seed of a bull. So she goes off to the butcher's. These sexual changes in cows happen during droughts and periods of poor grazing. Poverty and misery cause similar changes in human beings—as in the case of Germany after the First World War. Women are far easier to corrupt and more liable to vice when they are poor or starving. The same happens with cows.

There are three kinds of *cabestros*—stirrup *cabestros*, in pairs, who go on each side of the *vaquero*: horse *cabestros*, who go singly behind the *vaquero* at the horse's tail: and *troop-cabestros*, who are trained to surround the cattle they are conducting. All these in their various evolutions perform a function analogous, though not similar to those of sheep-dogs in the herding of sheep.

The lance, or *garrocha*, or trident, is used much from the ground in Spain by dismounted cattle-men, but in Portugal and France it is used equally by dismounted as by mounted cattle-men. They are especially good at deflecting the charge of a bull by kneeling with the haft under one foot and aiming the points of the lance or trident into the nose of the bull: as he ricochets off and blunders past, the man takes the same position again, facing about, but changing only the direction in which he aims. The bull soon finds out that it is no use and goes off, licking the blood from his nose.

Young cows are proved in the *tientas* by a very heavy grilling from the picadors. The young bulls are not given such treatment, though they are sometimes tested with the cape or with dummy figures. They are tested when they are branded: the cowards go to the butcher. This is because it might make them suspicious and reserved in their final entry into the arena. But a conscientious breeder will always test his young cows to the full.

CHAPTER SEVEN

Portuguese Poetry
from King Sancho I to José Regio

PORTUGAL WAS already a nation with its own language before the twelfth century began. The next century was spent in the expulsion of the Moors (who bequeathed 700 words to the Portuguese language) from the southern half of the country, and in the separation of the whole country from that of Spanish Galicia in the north, where almost the same language as Portuguese is spoken to this day. The Galicians and Portuguese were mingled and crossed with the invading Goths in the north: yet their music, dances, and tartans resemble those of the Scottish and Irish: and in the north the bagpipe has not yet been ousted by the guitar. The Celtic language disappeared throughout the whole peninsula since, owing to certain affinities with the language of the early Roman conquerors and colonists, it was easily assimilated by them. In spite of the loss of the Gaelic language, Portuguese poetry is innately Celtic. Of the languages primitively spoken on the Peninsula, only the Basque remains ruggedly intact, partly owing to its dissimilarity from almost all known languages, and the consequent difficulty of assimilating it by modification. The Gaelic languages always survive longest, as in Britain and Ireland, when Teutons or Scandinavians are the invaders, since they remain insoluble in the more alien element for a longer time.

Some local Portuguese peasant words for birds and animals are identical with Gaelic words for the same animals—but apart from these, few other traces remain of the old Celtiberian tongue.

When Portuguese and Galician were indistinguishably one language—that is, before the imperial rôle of Portugal developed and complicated the former language as the instrument of a vast civilization with a world-wide mission—that single language, next to the Provençal tongue, then current in all the royal courts of Europe, was the leading living poetical language of the Middle Ages. Many fine poets within the Spanish borders have continued to write in Galician, in preference to Castilian, down to modern times, as in the case of the popular Spanish poetess Rosalia de Castro, who is loved equally by Portuguese and Galician readers. That great Portuguese scholar, Aubrey Bell, included her work in his famous *Oxford Book of Portuguese Verse*, though subsequent editors removed it along with that of the other Galician, Eduardo Pondal, and the Brazilian, Olavo Bilac, in order to make room for purely Portuguese writers, though they still include that greatest of all foreign writers of Portuguese, King Don Alfonso the Tenth (surnamed 'the Wise') of Castile, who is a great Portuguese poet in his own right. In modern times the Andalusian poet Garcia Lorca tried to write several poems in Galician. Though these were failures, they were at least a tribute to the historical prestige of the language.

That a king of this great and powerful kingdom should have chosen to write his immortal poetry in this foreign language, in preference to his own lovely Castilian, is a measure of the pre-eminence that was then accorded to the Lusitanian Gallego–Portuguese language. Almost without exception the European monarchs of the Middle Ages wrote passable and sometimes fine poetry in the Provençal language. It was part of a royal education along with equitation, swordsmanship, and Latin—to write Provençal verse. That of the English king, Edward the Second, is truly fine, and far superior to the much-vaunted efforts of Richard Cœur de Lion. Both of them wrote their best work in prison, but the robust lion-heart of the latter seems to have handicapped him from reaching the poignancy and pathos expressed by the former's more sensitive and delicate nature. When we compare the poems in Provençal ascribed to Alfonso the Wise, to those he wrote in Portuguese, and to the noble foundations of Castilian prose laid by the same great man, the superiority of both these languages becomes apparent, and we are not surprised that both, in their subsequent poetry and prose, should by so far have over-towered the original literary language, which was the precursor, in nearly every civilized European country, of its own indigenous literature.

Portugal was no exception to the rule, in that the first lyrical poetry written by Portuguese poets was all in Provençal. But Portugal differed from the other races of Europe in that the first poetry to appear in her own tongue was not a primitive epic like the *Poem of the Cid*, *Beowulf*, the *Chanson de Roland*, the *Nibelungenlied*, or the sagas with which the literatures of the Spaniards, the English, the Germans, and the Scandinavians began.

Most of these literatures started with an epic river-spate of song: and many of them, to judge by much modern verse, are threatening to peter out in inert, stagnant puddles of obscurity and ambiguity. Portuguese poetry, on the contrary, began like the noble rivers on whose banks it was written, the Mondego, the Douro, the Tagus, and the Minho, as a pure and crystalline source of refreshing, shining, and musical lyricism—as unliterary and seemingly effortless as the song of birds or cicadas. Like the Tagus, it has continued to grow deeper and wider, and after forming one big lake in Camões and Gil Vicente, in the golden age, as the Tagus does at Vila Franca, continues to flow with strength and abundance in the modern verse of Pessoa, Teixeira de Pascoaes, José Regio, and the rest of the modern pleiad.

Even in its own home in Provence, the Provençal poetry of the early troubadours was as unnatural, over-cultivated, super-literary, artificial, and affected as the loves it celebrated and the vices it tried to deodorize with paper flowers. To me the recent and modern Provençal poetry of Mistral, Aubanel, Jasmin, Baroncelli, and d'Arbaud is worth that of all the old troubadors put together. The first Portuguese poetry was in its very essence a revolt against the artificial formality imposed by the Provençal models, though this applies only to lyrical poetry. The *satirical* poetry in the Provençal tongue known as the *cantigas de maldiʒer* (comparable to the lowland 'flytings' of Dunbar and Kennedy) was nearly always full of lively humour and energy. It was the love-songs in Provençal, the *cantigas de amor*, that were over-literary, insipid, stereotyped, and monotonous: vitality seemed to be sacrificed to technical correctness in over-elaborate rhyme-schemes and verse-forms.

However in the songs of *maldiʒer* (or *evil-speaking*), as in modern scurrility, limericks, or epigrams, the difficulty of the sheer technical performance, the strictness and intricacy of the form, the complexity of the metre and rhyme, all enhance rather than detract from the artistic success of the poem. It would seem that no aid is too artificial: no antithetical shock or surprise, within the bounds of wit, too incongruous: no distortion or exaggeration too disproportionate for successful satire, and the poetry of hate. Where a poem expressing love can lose through too much technical virtuosity, neatness of wit, precision and dexterity, clearness of outline, aptness of metaphor, and anything even faintly approaching, in onomatapoeia, to the kisses, sighs, cries, tears, groans, or raptures of love—a poem expressing hate, on the contrary, profits by every one of these forms of artifice which (if we make the one exception of love poetry) are the very stuff of which *all* poetry is made, not only satire, but narrative, descriptive, philosophical, and especially epic poetry, which, by reason of its length and consequent threat of monotony, cannot be too highly seasoned with spices, illuminated with fireworks, illustrated with highly coloured imagery, and varied with changing music.

The Galician language owed its pre-eminence in the mediæval world to the fact that thousands of pilgrims, soldiers, priests, and knights from all over Christendom for centuries visited Santiago de Compostela, in Galicia. At the same time there was a constant immigration into Galicia and Portugal from France. Many crusaders settled in Portugal on their way to, or home from, the Holy Land: others found they could fight the infidel as conveniently in Portugal as farther afield, and remained as settlers on the lands they wrested from the Moors. This accounts for the fact that, though Portugal is on the farther side of Spain from France, there is a much closer affinity between French and Galician–Portuguese, than with any of the Spanish languages spoken nearer France, such as Catalan, Valencian, Castilian, or Basque. The popularity of the shrine of the Apostle Saint James at Compostela rivalled that of St. Peter's in Rome, and among the pilgrims were many famous poets from the noble, highborn *trovador* to the humble *segrel*, and the ragged *jogral*, who were all also to be found amongst the permanent, stationary population. So great was the traffic to Santiago, that people believed that the Milky Way had no other purpose than to point the way there.

The *cossante* or lyric of parallel verses has no counterpart in any other language than Gallego–Portuguese. It was the medium of the Portuguese troubadors. This literature was lost sight of by the conscious baroque artists of the Renaissance, as being too rustic, naive, and artless. It remained for modern scholars to unearth the priceless treasures of the *Cancioneiro da Vaticana*, *Cancioneiro Colocci Brancuti*, and *Cancioneiro da Ajuda*, three song-books which contain hundreds of beautiful lyrics.

A certain amount of influence on the *cossante* has been ascribed to the Arabic poetry of the south, but, as Aubrey Bell points out, the chief oriental strain in them derives from the psalms and hymns of church services. In tone and structure, however, they belong to the people. Each poem consists of two or more couplets with a refrain which repeats the sense, though often altering the sound. The only oriental effects reproduced in these poems will be seen to be Jewish rather than Moorish in their origin. They entirely lack the brilliant visual imagery of the Arab poets and depend mostly on musical effects. The repetitions common to both the psalms and to the Gaelic laments of the Hebrides will be found in these primitive songs, known as the *Cantigas de Amigo*. Here is one of the most famous and frequently anthologized of them.

Cantiga de Amigo

At St. Simeon's shrine I sat down to wait,
The waves came nearer, the waves grew great,
    As I was awaiting my lover,
    As I was awaiting my lover!
There at St. Simeon's shrine by the altar,
Greater and nearer, the waves did not falter,
    As I was awaiting my lover,
    As I was awaiting my lover!
As the waves drew nearer and greater grew,
There was no steersman nor rower in view,
    As I was awaiting my lover,
    As I was awaiting my lover!
The waves of the high sea nearer flow
There is no steersman, I cannot row
    As I am awaiting my lover,
    As I am awaiting my lover!
There is no steersman nor rower, and I
In the high sea in my beauty must die,
    As I am awaiting my lover,
    As I am awaiting my lover!
There is no steersman, no rower am I,
And in the high sea my beauty must die,
    As I am awaiting my lover,
    As I am awaiting my lover.

That is the sole surviving poem of the *jogral* Mindinho, probably a native of Vigo, since there is a shrine to Saint Simeon on an island in Vigo bay.

Here is a more sophisticated poem by Pero Meogo, another *iogral* who appears to have been a friar from his name (Peter Monk), but who writes love poetry with wonderful verve and freshness. You will often find allusions to stags and deer at the fountains in the poetry of that time. It was the commonest mendacious excuse of girls who had stayed out flirting when they went to fetch water (still today the chief duty of the daughter of the house) that they had been delayed at the fountain by waiting for it to clear after it had been made muddy by stags, goats, horses, cattle, or sheep drinking. Pero Meogo flourished in the twelfth century.

Cantiga de Amigo

(From the Galicean of Pero Meogo)

Tell me, my daughter, my pretty young daughter,
What kept you so long at the fountain for water?
(I've fallen in Love)
Tell me my daughter, my beautiful thing,
What caused you to linger beside the cold spring?
(I've fallen in Love)
I loitered, dear mother, so long by the fountain
For stags had been coming to drink from the mountain.
(I've fallen in Love)
I waited so long for the water to clear
Because it was churned into mud by the deer.
(I've fallen in Love)
You are lying, my girl, for your lover, I think:
Since I saw no stag coming down to the brink.
(I've fallen in Love)
You are lying, my daughter, for love it must be,
For I never saw stag which could trouble the Sea.
(I've fallen in Love)

Here is another poem by Pero Meogo:

My lover goes wounded
And by my love struck
As by the king's keeper
Goes wounded a buck.
Oh mother, he goes,
By my love struck deeper
Than a buck wounded
By the head-keeper.
To drown in the sea
Goes the buck that is shot:
So will my friend
If I think of him not.

—Be guarded, my daughter,
I've seen such, with art,
Feigning for pity
To soften the heart.
Be guarded, my daughter,
I've known such, with skill,
Feigning for pity
To weaken the will.

The *trovadores, jograles,* and *segreles* always wrote in set forms, of which the commonest were the following: *cantigas de amor, cantigas de amigo,* which are all love-songs: *bailadas,* dance-songs, danced to by peasants at country festivals: *barcarolas,* or boat-songs: *albas,* or dawn-songs, sung to awaken one's mistress: *marinas,* and *cantigas de ria,* or songs of the sea: *cantigas de romaria,* songs of pilgrimage: *serranilhas,* pastoral songs for shepherds in the mountains. The Cantigas de Santa Maria are a series of beautiful hymns written to the Virgin by King Alfonso the Wise. The *cantiga de amigo,* or song of the male friend, was always put in the mouth of a girl in love. Here is a *bailada* by Airas Nunes, a twelfth-century *trovador*:

Bailada

Come let us dance, my friends, all three,
Under the flowering hazel tree,
For whoever is fair, as fair as we,
    If she have a lover,
Only the flowering hazel tree
    Will ever discover.

Dance now, my sisters, dance all three
Under this branch of the hazel tree,
For whoever is fine, as fine as we,
    If she have a lover,
Only this branch of the hazel tree
    Will ever discover.

By God, my friends, when there's naught else chancing,
Under this hazel tree come dancing.
For whoever looks well, as we look now,
If she have a lover,
Only the overshadowing bough
Will ever discover.

After Pai Soares de Taveiros, who wrote the first poetical document in the Portuguese language, King Sancho I seems to be the earliest poet to have written in it. But it is King Dinis who should really be called the father of Portuguese poetry, for in all his verse pulses and vibrates the ardour of plenary inspiration, though it is often homely and popular in style, like the verse of Burns or Dunbar. One of his loveliest songs is on the humble theme of a pretty girl going out to wash shirts and the wind blowing them all away, and leaving her furious on the hillside—but it is, alas, quite untranslatable: the bloom goes from it like the dust from a butterfly's wing the moment one handles it. King Alfonso, the Wise, was also democratic in his love of simple fisher-folk, monks, nuns, peasants, and labourers. The great difference in the Portuguese love-poems from those of Provence is in the fact that they appear to be inspired solely by love. The poet does not attitudinize in a mirror, as many Provençaux do, and we never learn from him what sort of situation or social triangle his love involves him in. We are not told whether the inspirer of his poems is married or single, rich or poor; such details are beneath the whole-hearted devotion that preoccupies most of the Portuguese *trovadores*, of whom about sixty-three are included in Vitorino Nemésio's recent collection, with a very fine introduction. The *trovadores* dated from the twelfth to the fifteenth century, when there was suddenly a great silence following the death of King Dom Dinis.

The most famous names among the Portuguese troubadors are Joan Zorro, Martin Codax, Pero Meogo, Juan Bolsero, Airas Nunes, Joan de Lobeira, Pai Gomez Charinho, King Alfonso, and King Dinis. A *jogral* wrote '*nunca pois de as morte trobaron*' referring to the death of Dom Dinis: 'no one wrote poems after

his death'. It would seem that the silence that followed was one
of mourning; perhaps it was partly due to the lack of such
munificent royal patrons to reward the *jograles* and *segreles* with
enough money to live on.

At this time the Castilian influence began to make itself felt
and many fine Portuguese poets began to use Castilian in preference to their own tongue. Never were Portugal and Castile
nearer to a peaceful union than then, for though they were
united under a single crown later, it was not a union of harmony.

The Spanish romances or ballads were imitated by Portuguese
poets in Spanish, since that language was considered proper for
that metre: and it was thus that some of the Spanish ballads
acquired a lovely, melancholy tenderness which is alien to their
direct, dramatic verve and strength in the hands of the native
Spanish writers.

In 1516 the poet Garcia de Resende published a vast compendium of the works of some two hundred poets in Portuguese
and Castilian. Much of this collection was artificial and common-
place. Italian influence, working through the great Spanish poet,
the Marquis of Santillana, could be seen in the work of Garcia de
Resende and Francisca de Sousa. The latter wrote a finely
pathetic, long poem on the death of Ines de Castro which has
inspired more fine poetry and sculpture than almost any other
event in Portuguese history.

Garcia de Resende was rather a poet of the Court than of the
people, and, except in this fine poem, is more a scholar than a
genius. It was the great Portuguese victory of Aljubarrota over
the Spanish in 1385 that restored the prestige of the Portuguese
language, but most of the literary activity was in prose, not
poetry, the most remarkable achievement being the superb
historical chronicles of Fernam Lopes.

The popular reawakening of a national spirit was intensified by
the discoveries in Africa, Asia, and America, when every fisherman or ploughman might turn into a conquistador, and everyone
dreamed of adventure, triumph, wealth, and power. This
popular awakening found expression in one of the two supreme

Setúbal

Market day at Guimaraes

Edgar Ritchard

Above, left to right—Fisherfolk of Nazare—Fisher boys in Albufeira—Girls of Nazare

geniuses of Portuguese literature, Gil Vicente, a sturdy son of the soil with abundant humour, great strength, and an inspired lyrical gift. He was a sort of Breughel, in verse, and his plays are full of deep wisdom, ragged gaiety, sound sense, coarse realism, and horseplay, interspersed with some of the most beautiful songs in any language. When occasion required he could write equally well in Castilian as in Portuguese. He often reminds one of Chaucer in his humour. Beneath his gaiety however he is a stern moralist. Here is the translation of a scene from one of his plays:

What Every-Man does, and what No-one does

SCENE: Two Devils, Dinato and Belzebub.

BEL: To get an estimate for sending
To Lucifer, our God and King,
Sit here and write down everything
We notice in the period pending—
For now the world is near its ending,
And that we may deserve our due
In the share-out, we must review,
And make a decent list, compending
All things that happen in our view.

(*Enter Every-Man—a man dressed as a rich merchant and looking around, as if for something he has lost. Then, after him, enter a man dressed as a pauper, whose name is No-one.*)

NO-ONE: What are you so intent to find?

EVERY-MAN: I go to seek a thousand things
Whose getting never eased my mind—
Still striving in persistence never brings.

NO-ONE: What is your name, sir, and your role?

EVERY-MAN: My name is Every-Man. My whole
Existence is in seeking wealth.
This task employs my time and health
And is the function of my soul.

NO-ONE: My name is No-one. My one goal
Is conscience.

BEL: Put that down in style
And with a flourish. It's so funny!

I

DIN:	Comrade, how shall I word the file?
BEL:	'No-one follows his conscience, while Every-Man hunts around for money.'
NO-ONE:	What now, sir, would you seek to see?
EVERY-MAN:	My name renowned through all the land.
NO-ONE:	I seek for virtue—as for me. And, look! I have it here to hand, As if it were by God's decree.
BEL:	Another item. Note the same. These very words at once insert you!— That 'Every-Man goes chasing Fame, But No-one chases after Virtue.'
NO-ONE:	No other blessing would you claim?
EVERY-MAN:	Why, yes—that one and all should praise My slightest action, deed, or venture!
NO-ONE:	And I—that one and all should censure The slightest error in my ways.
BEL:	Write more!
DIN:	But how would you have penned it?
BEL:	That 'even to the extremest measure Every-Man in his praise takes pleasure, No-one in being reprehended!'
EVERY-MAN:	I seek long life, and all who give it.
NO-ONE:	I do not know, although I live it, What life is. Death is all I know.
BEL:	Record that in a different breath.
DIN:	How?
BEL:	Why, far more waggishly and gaily! That 'Life by Every-Man is daily Pursued, while No-one thinks of Death.'
EVERY-MAN:	I long for Paradise, with no Disturbance to my peace and joy.
NO-ONE:	I long in penance to employ My soul—to pay the debt I owe.
BEL:	Put that one down, and be precise.
DIN:	The words, then?
BEL:	This is how it goes: 'While Every-Man wants paradise, No-one would pay the debt he owes.'

EVERY-MAN: I love to do a bit of cheating.
                Lying was born with me, I guess.
NO-ONE: The truth is what I love repeating—
                And never from its path digress.
BEL: Comrade, note that one down entire
                Quick, get it down, and don't be lazy!
DIN: What?
BEL: Write down that 'Every-Man's a liar,
                But No-one for the truth is crazy!'
EVERY-MAN: I love to fawn, and cringe, and flatter.
NO-ONE: For me such things are no great matter.
                I've no illusions on that score.
BEL: Write it!
DIN: But how to phrase the patter?
BEL: Quick! Mark it clearly to our score—
                And goggle at the ink no more!—
                That 'Every-Man delights to flatter,
                But No-one finds it all a bore.'

In his range of characters Gil Vicente was almost Shake-spearean, for he produces idealized kings and heroes with the same skill as he produces the lower types. In his *Autos* or religious plays he reveals a profoundly religious, and therefore Portuguese, spirit. He reaches his greatest height in the trilogy of *The Ship of Hell*, *The Ship of Purgatory*, and *The Ship of Paradise*. The last of these was written in Castilian, but has been very well translated by Professor Paulo Quintela. In this trilogy Gil Vicente antici-pates the imperial epic poetry of the *Lusiads* of Camões, for he calls up the ghosts of the Fidalgos of the Order of Christ, who died in the African crusades. The Devil questions them thus when they enter the other world:

SATAN: Knights, do you dare to pass me thus,
             Without declaring whither bound?
1ST KNIGHT: Who do you think you are, Mahound
             That you presume to speak with us?
2ND KNIGHT: Satan, what do you ask about?
             You know us well beyond a doubt.

We died upon a distant shore.
With that, you need enquire no more.

ANGEL: (*intervening*)

Awaiting here for you was I,
O chevaliers of God on high,
You who have perished in the war
For Christ, the Lord of all the sky.
You are exempted from all pain
As saints for certain without stain,
Since all who perished in that strife
Merit eternal peace and life.

We deal elsewhere with Gil Vicente's genius as a painter and sculptor-goldsmith of the Cellini class. He is the greatest all-round original genius that Portugal ever produced, and if he yields an inch to Camões in the sphere of poetry, it is due to the latter's powers of assimilation and learning from classical and contemporary foreign models. Here is a song from Gil Vicente literally translated, without attempting the impossible, which would be to try to capture the charm along with the meaning, which is as follows:

Rowing go the rowers
In a ship of great delight.
The captain at the helm
The Son of God is Light.
Angels at the oars
Rowed with all their might.
The flag of hope was flying
Lovely to the sight.
The mast was of endurance
Like crystal shining bright.
The sails were stitched with faith
And filled the world with light.
The seashore was serene
With not a wind in flight.

When Philip II of Spain later became king of Portugal, there was another last threat to the sovereignty of the Portuguese language, but it was largely forestalled by the arrival, in 1526, of the learned Sá de Miranda from Italy with a sound knowledge of Italian poetry, bringing with him new forms such as the *terza rima* and the sonnet, until then untried in Portugal. Thus a new impetus was given to Portuguese verse that subsequently resisted the years of Spanish rule. The contemporaries and disciples of Miranda, Don Manuel de Portugal, Diogo Bernardes, Cristovam Falcam, Antonio Ferreira,[1] Bernadim Ribeiro, and Francisco Sáde Menezes all wrote delightful bucolic poetry, eclogues for the most part, but free from the artifice of Vergilian imitations. King Dom Sebastian took the smoothly melodious Bernardes with him, on the suicidal and disastrous expedition in which he and the flower of the Portuguese aristocracy died fighting at Alcacer Kibir. Bernardes, who had been taken there by the king in order that he might versify his exploits as an eye-witness, lived only to lament his master's death and his own captivity. He was one of the mere fifty wounded who survived this disaster as a prisoner of the Moors, to be ransomed years later. His sorrows and hardships never succeeded in ruffling the mellifluous harmonies of his verse.

Bernardes' friend and fellow-countryman from the Alentejo, Cristovam Falcam, wrote more vigorously and vitally than the former in his famous *Trovas de Crisfal*; but all these poets were eclipsed by their greatest contemporary, Luiz de Camões, who is equally great whether as a lyrical poet or an epic poet. Once he had written, the Portuguese language was safe for ever. The greatest Spaniards—Lope,[2] Gongora, Cervantes, Calderon, Tirso de Molina, Quevedo, and others—looked up to him, and wrote of him as their superior. His contemporaries of the Miranda Pleiad seem to have been ignorant of his existence or, if not, they left him in the splendid isolation of genius.

The Portuguese are the only people to have a word which

---

[1] Antonio Ferreira wrote a great tragedy on Inés de Castro, an innovation in that it did not go to the old Greeks for a subject, and a triumph of dramatic force; the blank verse at times recalls Shakespeare or Webster.

[2] Lope in his *Laurel de Apolo* even goes as far as to praise the *Lusiads* above the epics of antiquity.

exactly hits off that sense of brooding exile, a sort of homesickness
which can even be felt at home, that otherwise undefinable fusion
of yearning with satisfaction, pain with pleasure, and resignation
with unattainability—which is the keynote of their poetry, and
which the word *saudade* conveys so perfectly, as does no other
word in any other language. It is the 'smiling regret' of Baudelaire's wonderfully sad and beautiful line in *Receuillement*

> Surgir du fond des eaux le regret souriant . . .

and again in de Nerval's

> Le prince d'Aquitaine à la tour abolie

It is made of the very

> . . . foam
> Of perilous seas in faery lands forlorn.

which the lonely Portuguese mariners were the first to explore
before they had lost the wonderment and weirdness of a legendary
world, a world in which their losses by shipwreck, hunger, disease
and hardship were so many that the greatest of modern Portuguese poets, Pessoa, in one of his maritime poems, says that the
very salt of the sea is from the tears of the wives, mothers, and
sweethearts of Portuguese sailors and fishermen, who have waited
in suspense for their unreturning sons, or lovers. This sense of
suspense is in the very blood of the Portuguese, and it intensifies
the original grave melancholy of which it is a natural projection.
The nearest thing we have to it in Britain is to be found in the
border ballads, and certain Gaelic and Jacobite songs, all of
which derive their *flavour* from an equally high death-rate from
unnatural causes. It is present in the anonymous Canadian Boat
Song of the exiled Highlanders and is redolent of 'old unhappy
far-off times and battles long ago':

> From the lone shieling of the misty island
> Mountains divide us and a waste of seas,
> But still the blood is strong, the heart is Highland,
> And we in dreams behold the Hebrides.

It is no mere coincidence either that a quarter of the early Portuguese poems are *barcarolas* or boat-songs, like those of the Hebridean fishermen.

But the nostalgia we feel most deeply in Portuguese poetry (from the earliest *barcarolas*) is less perhaps a nostalgia of place than of time, remembrance, and hope. Perhaps the finest poem in Portuguese is the great poem Camões wrote on the theme of the Babylonian Captivity which expresses not only the yearning of a common soldier in a remote outlandish Asiatic garrison, but his regrets for happy times and lost friends, and, above all, his longing hopes as a Christian for a better world to come.

Camões, in his lineage, education, and life, incorporated everything that goes to the making of the best poetry. His male ancestry went back to the noble cattle-raising stock of Galicia from which he derived his poetic talent from the trovador Perez Camões, his direct ancestor, whose poems have been lost. His Celtic blood was tempered by later admixtures of a more sober *gothic* type, by which he derived that wonderful sense of balance, discipline, and structure which is necessary to an epic poet. Without it a great genius like Blake (an Irish Celt by descent) can make random soaring flights, but can sustain no towering effort in structure, speed, and strength, like the *Lusiads*, which rushes along like a great Atlantic liner through calm and storm alike, with the same steady pulse of the turbine. Camões, though he had a splendid University education, appears to have spent his childhood as an orphan in the wilds of the Ribatejo where he tells us bitterly that instead of mother's milk, he was nourished on that of a 'fierce wild animal'—meaning probably one of the fighting breed of cattle.

> When my unhappy stars decreed my birth
> From the maternal womb upon this Earth,
> A wild beast was my nurse. By fates' decree
> No woman ever bore that name for me.

This symbolic and almost mythical detail tallies with the rest of Camões's fantastically sad story. One could hardly believe it if there were not such parallels as the demagogue Danton who was suckled by a cow (though a domestic one) and savaged by a bull whose jealousy he apparently aroused, so that he bore the marks on his face till his dying day, and could never, for long after, refrain from throwing stones at bulls. I have seen Spanish, Zulu, and Afrikaner children suckling from goats and cows, so I find it easy enough to credit. It is fitting, in view of what we have said of the *saudade* being the keynote of Portuguese poetry, that the greatest of Portuguese poets should have been also one of the Portuguese who suffered the longest exile and the worst misfortunes, to die an unknown beggar, blind in the streets of Lisbon, and friendless save for his faithful Bantu slave, who now lies buried at the foot of his sumptuous tomb next to Vasco da Gama's in the Jeronimos Church at Belem on the outskirts of Lisbon.

At the outbreak of the last war I sailed from Lisbon to volunteer for the British Army, and spent all the money I had on the complete poems of Camões, which I eventually carried in my kit-bag round the Cape and out east to many of the very places described in the Lusiads, such as Mombaça, Melinde, Lama: but the most extraordinary coincidence was to be posted, when unfit for more active service, opposite the very spot where he wrote the most affecting of his *Canções*; apparently he was coast-watching for Arab dhows, as I was for Jap submarines, which often camouflaged themselves as dhows, to come in close, as did the one that loosed an aeroplane over Mombaça—which joy-rode round the town for quite a time without being fired at.

The 'hideous mountain' of Camões is at Cape Guardafui. Although my exile was tempered by the splendid company of both Camões and Baudelaire, and the weekly visit of a launch with my whisky ration and a newspaper, it was a grim place. A poet can stand more than a philosopher, but a lighthouse-keeper is supposed to be able to stand twice as much boredom and loneliness as a poet and a philosopher put together: yet so terribly barren is this place that my nearest neighbour, the lighthouse-keeper on Cape Guardafui, went clean off his head, raving and fighting mad with loneliness; so Major Mahoney of the Intelligence Corps got me to tie him up and ship him on the launch. I never heard whether he recovered on reaching civilization. I passed the time there translating this famous *Canção* from Camões in full view of the scenes he describes, with a squad of black *askaris* of the King's African Rifles, some of whom had filed teeth and others ears like rifle-slings, so that they had to be tied round the upper cartilages of their ears before parades, lest they should stick their rifles through their own ears when sloping arms! It was the right human as well as the right geographical environment in which to appreciate this poem. 'The wild native in his savage tongue' was quite as eloquent as in Camões time: but they were good fellows.

Canção IX

There is a mountain, sterile, stark and dry,
Useless, abandoned, hideous, bare and bald,
From whose cursed precincts nature shrinks appalled,
Where no beast ever sleeps, where no birds fly,
No river runs, nor bubbling sources spring,
Nor one green bough with pleasant sighs to sing.
In common speech the name they call it by
Is Felix [1] (unfelicitously given!)
By Nature it was placed
Just where a strait has riven
The Arabian from the Abyssinian waste,
Where Berenice used to stand of yore,
In that part of the shore
Where the sun, having burnt it, hides once more;

Thence can be seen the Cape which ends the coast
Of Africa, which runs up from the south,
Called 'Aromatic' by as vain a boast
But something far less flowery in the mouth
Of the wild native in his savage tongue.
(Though fragrant once, perhaps, when time was young.)

[1] Arabia Felix.

There by the sea, whose high tide-swollen spate
Strives twice a day to burst that narrow strait,
To languish for a spell
It was my cursed fate,
There in that fierce inhospitable hell,
Where Life would fain desert itself to see
Its splintered bits, ah me!
Scattered about the world by land and sea.

Here was I stranded, passing dreary days,
Laborious evil, dolorous days and lonely,
Days full of toil, grief, rage, and long delays—
Not having for my adversaries only
Life, and the burning sun, and the chill tides,
With fierce, hot, roaring hurricanes besides,
But my own thoughts which only seemed my own
To play foul tricks on nature and deceive.
My memory too had grown
A thing to make me grieve,
Reviving some brief glories I had known
When in the world I sojourned, so to double,
By contrast, all my suffering and trouble,
By keeping me aware
That in the world were long hours free from care.

There did I live wasting both life and time
With these vain thoughts, which to a height immense
Reared me so steeply on their wings to climb
That so much steeper was my fall from thence,
Dashed downward from those castles in the air
To reach whose height I ever more despair.
Imagination here was turned to grief
In unexpected sobs to find relief
And sighs which rent the air.
My captive spirit there,
Wounded all over to the tender quick,
Crowded all round with sorrows dense and thick,
Unshielded lay beneath the hailing shot
Of my accursed lot,
Inexorable, fierce, and hell-begot.

There was not anywhere the least relief,
Nor any hope whereon to lay my head
And snatch a little rest, however brief.
All things for harm and suffering seemed bred
Save that I could not die: for to have died
Would baulk my angry fate, and was denied.
My groans made calm the stormy waves that rolled,
Importuned by my voice, the winds grew cold
Worn out with my lament.
Only the heavens cruel,
The stars, and fate, so fierce in its intent,
Found their amusement in the oft-renewal
Of my sad torments, showing off their spite
My wretched self to smite,
Poor earthly thing, and such a tiny mite!

O that amongst these labours I might only
Know that for certain I shall once behold,
But for one hour, two eyes I knew of old:
That my lament, so desolate and lonely,
Might reach the ears of that angelic sprite
Within whose view I lived in such delight:
And that she, turning backward in her mind,
Might, thinking of the times we've left behind,
Recall each sweet mistake,
Quarrel, or torment kind
I sought and suffered only for her sake:
And thus, remembering such things, were she
To feel a pang for me
And her own stony-heartedness to see:

Only to know this thing would mean, for me,
Peace through the rest of life that yet remains.
With that I could console my dreary pains.
Ah, Lady, Lady! Wealthy you must be
Since even to imagine you sustains,
Far from all pleasures, what remains of me
When in my thoughts your effigy I see
All pain and weariness turn tail and flee.

Alone your memory arms
My soul with fearless might
Against ferocious death and mortal harms.
New hopes come rushing to me from your charms,
New hopes, with which my brow serenely bright
Confronts the woes I fight
Turning them into memories of delight.

Here with these memories I remain, and sue
Of every amorous zephyr of the air
From your part of the world, some news of you.
I ask the birds which seem to fly from there
If they have seen you, when, and what you do,
What day and hour it was, with whom, and where.
Thus my tired life from day to day improves:
I win new spirits: something in me moves
Which conquers toil and fate
To feel that once again
I may return to see you at some date,
To love, and serve, and with you to remain.
Say when the time will come that ends my pain!
But my desire, that nothing can abate,
Pitiless as before,
Has opened up my suffering wounds once more.

Thus live I. If they ask you, Song, why I
Have not yet chance to die,
Tell them that I am dying: That is why.

Speaking of Camões, in her monumental *Life and Works of
Camões*, Dona C. Michaëlis says: 'The quantity and density of
scientific knowledge in the works of Camões causes astonishment,
principally in consideration of the fact that voluminous libraries
were so rare and the cost of manuscripts and printed codices so
high as to make it very difficult even to use books, let alone
acquire them. But we must admire his prodigious memory even
more, and the way in which he used his vast knowledge of
universal history, geography, astronomy, classical mythology,

ancient and modern literatures, learned and popular poetry, of
Italy as well as of Spain, employing it with the most perfect
exactitude, as a legitimate son of the Renaissance and one of the
most learned and outstanding humanists of his time.' To
illustrate his mastery of popular forms here is a translation of one
of his little poems in Spanish:

The Sailor-Girl

Mother, my sighs unfurl
Forth on the seas to sally
With one in yonder galley
To be a sailor-girl.

O Mother mine, if only
I were where I would go!
I hate this Love so lonely,
This Love that loves him so,
This Cupid who's a churl,
This Babe who is my gaoler,
This longing for a sailor—
To be a sailor-girl!

He who all knots unravels
One he cannot unbind—
That though the spirit travels
The body stays behind.
With him for whom I'm dying
I'll go (or die—you'll see!)
All for a sailor trying
A sailor-girl to be.

What a despotic thing
The Tyrant Babe decreed
That One who is a King
For Love should have to bleed!
In such a wise, ah me!
Daily do I grow paler
For one who is a sailor
A sailor-girl to be.

> Say, waves, if yet before
> You ever saw so slender
> A maiden, or so tender,
> Go smiling from the shore!
> From Babes that act the Demon
> What mischiefs are not due?
> To travel with my seaman
> I'll be a sailor too!

There was no form, whether native and popular, whether imported and literary, in which Camões did not excel those whom he imitated, from the eight-lined verses of Ariosto, Tasso, and Boiardo, to the *canzoni* and sonnets of Petrarch. Though in his invocation to the *Lusiads* he solemnly consigns other poets to more light-hearted themes, yet when he wishes to he can out-skylark even Ariosto, as when, in the Ninth Book of the *Lusiads*, he suddenly becomes dionysiacally playful and takes a holiday. There is nothing in his models to equal the terrifying grandeur of the apparition of the Spirit of the Cape of Good Hope, as the Giant Adamastor, or the prophetic truth of his allocution to the Portuguese argonauts of Vasco da Gama as they round the Cape of Storms for the first time. There is nothing in his models to equal the tender pathos of Camões's reference to Ines de Castro in the Lusiads. Passages like those describing the fighting at Melinde, the storms, the rounding of the Cape, and the South Sea islands certainly owe as much to his experience as a soldier and a sailor as they do to his reading. As well could Melville have written *Moby Dick* without the experience as Camões the *Lusiads*. Here it is interesting to compare him with a great Spanish contemporary, a soldier too, who wrote a famous epic almost entirely from experience. Ercilla, the Spanish poet of the *Araucana*, has been compared sometimes to Camões, and generally to his disfavour.

Camões (together with him) is the soldier's poet *par excellence*. But they should not be compared to either's discredit. They are so different. Ercilla is made of iron. He is the poet to carry in a hard-hitting war like the Spanish Civil War, where the delays are fewer, the military action more sustained, and one's reading has to be more concentrated. When he was writing those iron cantos of the *Araucana*, on sheepskins, by camp-fires in the freezing altitudes of the Andes, Ercilla had no words to spare for beauty, or personal regret, or anything but the drama in hand. But Camões is the one to enchant stagnant, dead hours in malarial swamps, or endless dusty days on desert promontories, and after a couple of years with him, I wrote the following sonnet to express the real comradeship he finally inspires: it expresses that feeling better than could be done in prose.

> Camões, alone of all the lyric race,
> Born in the angry morning of disaster
> Can look a common soldier in the face.
> I find a comrade where I sought a master
> For daily, while the stinking crocodiles
> Glide from the mangroves on the swampy shore,
> He shares my awning on the dhow, he smiles
> And tells me that he lived it all before.
> Through fire and shipwreck, pestilence and loss,
> Led by the *ignis fatuus* of duty
> To a dog's death—yet of his sorrows king—
> He shouldered high his voluntary Cross,
> Wrestled his hardships into forms of beauty,
> And taught his gorgon destinies to sing.

The *Lusiads* were nearly lost when Camões was shipwrecked in the Bay of Mecon, and had to swim, through stormy seas, for his life, carrying the manuscript in his hand, as Cæsar had to, with less danger, with his *Commentaries* at Alexandria. He appears to have been involved in some rebellion and suffered imprisonment. In Book VIII he tells us of his long career of bad luck.

> Enduring now of Neptune, now of Mars,
> The most inhuman perils and the scars,
> Like Canace, self-sentenced and undone,
> A pen in one hand, and a sword in one:

Now for my penury abhorred, evaded,
And now in foreign doss-houses degraded:
No sooner with a hope acquired, than straight
The deeper dashed from where I stood elate:
Now, with my life escaping on my back,
That hung upon a thread so thin and slack,
To save it was a miracle, no less
Than were our King for heathen to confess.
And yet, O Nymphs, these miseries, though great,
Suffice not to appease my angry fate,
Since all I've sung of others' woes and curses
Must be the prize and guerdon of my verses,
Replacing all the joys for which I yearn—
Honours, repose, and laurels: which to spurn,
New travails I have never proved before
Must be invented, and a thousand more.

Amongst the many scars he received in war was the loss of his right eye. The sonnet was Camões' most frequent form of expression. Of these three that follow in translation, the first is little known, but the other two sonnets are amongst his most famous.

On a shipmate, *Pero Moniz*, dying at Sea

My years on earth were short, but long for me,
And full of bitter hardship at the best:
My light of day sinks early in the sea:
Five lustres from my birth I took my rest.
Through distant lands and seas I was a ranger
Seeking some cure or remedy for life,
Which he whom Fortune loves not as a wife,
Will seek in vain through strife, and toil, and danger.
Portugal reared me in my green, my darling
Alanguer, but the dank, corrupted air
That festers in the marshes around there
Has made me food for fish here in the snarling,
Fierce seas that dark the Abyssinian shore,
Far from the happy homeland I adore.

Sonnet

Seven long years was Jacob herding sheep
For Laban, lovely Rachel's grim old father.
It was not for that mean old man, but rather
For her, he worked—the prize he longed to reap.
Days passed in expectation of one day.
That day of days became his sole idea.
But the old father swindled him with Leah
And gave him the wrong girl, with whom he lay.
The disillusioned shepherd, thus denied,
As if he'd never merited his bride,
Began another seven years' indenture.
Seven years more he laboured, staunch and strong,
Saying 'A longer contract I would venture—
But life's too short to serve a love so long.'

Sonnet

Dear gentle soul, who went so soon away
Departing from this life in discontent,
Repose in that far sky to which you went
While on this earth I linger in dismay.
In the ethereal seat where you must be,
If you consent to memories of our sphere,
Recall the love which, burning pure and clear,
So often in my eyes you used to see!
If then, in the incurable, long anguish
Of having lost you, as I pine and languish,
You see some merit—do this favour for me:
And to the God who cut your life short, pray
That he as early to your sight restore me
As from my own he swept you far away.

Camões said he wished to die with his country. It is true that Portugal suffered a long eclipse, both in literature and in worldly power, about the time of his death, but the immortal spirit of Camões has sustained her through her long decadence to her present recovery. What he is to the Portuguese populace may

K

be assessed in the fact that the only non-religious festival which is accorded the importance of one in Portugal is the Day of Camões. Imagine the English having a national holiday on 'Shakespeare Day'. They are awed by Shakespeare, but he is too aloof and impersonal to inspire a national love: he means nothing to *the people*. The nearest personal memory in England comparable to that of Camões in Portugal would be that of Lord Nelson. The Portuguese have as great sailors and as great a naval history as ours, but it would be difficult to imagine their celebrating a Vasco da Gama Day with the solemnity of a Camões Day. They put poetry first and, as Aubrey Bell says, the literature of the Portuguese is the greatest which a small nation has yet produced, with the exception of that of the ancient Greeks.

After the death of Camões, Francisco Manuel de Melo (1606–60) wrote one wonderful poem, the *Song of Babylon*, which rivalled even the supreme lyrical masterpiece of Camões, and was, like it, a paraphrase of the great Psalm of David. Both these Portuguese poems, especially Melo's, as well as their great original, must have been studied profoundly by Calderon in his towering *Auto, The Real and the Mystic Babylon*, which Verlaine in his famous sonnet classes as 'higher than Shakespeare', a verdict with which one can agree if one adds 'but not so deep'. Rodriguez Lobo was a derivative throwback to the bucolic and amorous poets of the previous century, but capable of passion and vehemence, and gifted with such technical skill as to be really charming as often as not. Two nuns, Soror Violante do Ceo and Soror Maria do Ceo, wrote excellent mystical verse which shows at times the Spanish influence of Gongora, who, though he ruined many of his imitators, was successfully assimilated by them.

The eighteenth century became a neo-classical desert dominated by the stucco figures of imitators of Horace and Pindar, one of whom, Diniz da Cruz e Silva, suddenly came to life with a lively comic satire, *O Hyssope*. The period is dominated by Filinto Elysio, the *nom de guerre* of F. M. do Nascimento who wrote stacks of faultless dull verse, but owed his chief popularity to having died of ill-treatment at the hands of the Marquis of Pombal, the masonic dictator who dominated the latter half of the century. One of these neo-classical poets, Pedro Antonio Correa, wrote a poem called the *Cantata de Dido*, and the admirers which he numbers to this day claim that but for the fashion of the times, he would have cut more than a secondary figure in Portuguese poetry.

The end of the century was enlivened by the satirical poet Nicolau Tolentino de Almeida, and even more so by the irruption of Bocage, the archetype of the revolutionary romantic poet of the nineteenth century. Hernâni Cidade calls him a 'pre-romantic', in that 'he made poetry his confidant'. He came as a volcanic explosion of all the native energies and traditions which had been petrified by the neo-classical period. His poetical works run into many volumes: a considerable amount of it, like that of Burns, is pornographic and circulates surreptitiously to this day. Only a very small percentage of what he wrote, since he was too erratic and spontaneous for solid work, has a lasting value, but that is absolutely deathless. He says of himself that he was the Aretine of his age. According to Beckford he alternately petrified and enchanted his hearers; his wit was inexhaustible, fantastic, and fabulous, and his character, even according to his own admission, ungovernable. His life was one of escapades, scrapes, eternal trouble with the strict censorship of Pombal, for which he suffered military exile abroad, and misfortunes of which a considerable portion seem to have been as justly deserved as Camões' were unjustly incurred. Not only did he have trouble with the masonic censorship, but fell foul of the Inquisition and was imprisoned in the Limoeiro or Lemon-Tree, as they call the Bastille of Lisbon. He died worn out with debauchery at the age of thirty-nine in a convent, warning all 'impious folk' not only to shun his errors but to tear up his works

> I was a second Aretine! I stained
> Sanctity! Impious folk, if you believe me,
> Tear up my verse! Believe eternal life!

The instability of his nature reminds one of Villon: at one moment he is mocking at all authority, and the next he is writing religious poetry. When, like Burns, he was trusted with work on the Excise, he fulfilled his duties as conscientiously as his Scottish contemporary, and could even write Miltonic or Wordsworthian sonnets on the colonial decadence of the nation, lashing out at corruption, or errors in administration. He will live by at least a dozen great sonnets of an almost epic quality—the one to Camões, that on the Decadence of the Empire, that on Town and Country Life, that beginning 'Quando na rósea nuvem', one or two love-sonnets, and lastly the one written on his deathbed, which opens a window into the great poetry of the post-romantics. Some of the lines prefigure Baudelaire's *Horloge*.

> My being turns to smoke in the mad strife
> Of passions which have whirled me in their wake.
> How miserably blind was I to take
> This human span for almost-endless life
> What countless suns the boastful fancy forges
> To gild this false existence as it flows,
> But now my slave-like nature undergoes
> The blasting havoc of a life of orgies.
>
> Pleasures, my tyrant cronies, in confusion,
> Hurling you to the gulf of disillusion,
> My thirsty soul no longer can be pent.
> Before my light fails, grant, my God! that I,
> (One moment saving what in years I spent),
> Who knew not how to live, learn how to die!

Almeida Garrett (b. 1799) was the first of the romantics proper. Like his English, French, and Spanish contemporaries, Byron, Shelley, Hugo, Lamartine, and Espronceda, whose influence he introduced, he went in for politics, but with more prominence and success, as orator, minister, and statesman, than any of them except Lamartine. With his great contemporary Alexandre Herculano, he landed with the foreign army of English and Frenchmen that finally chased King Dom Miguel from the throne of Portugal and reinstituted the long preponderance of liberalism under which the country sank during the rest of the century, losing not only the mighty empire of Brazil but a vast empire attaching the colony of Moçambique to that of Angola, which, though belonging to Portugal by treaty, was surrendered to the British when the latter threatened war. Garrett is generally considered the best poet of the half-century ending in 1850. He was also the leading dramatist, essayist, and prose-writer. His poetry is not of the kind that can be translated by a modern author. We are nearer in mood, if not in performance, to previous and later periods: but this does not detract in any way from that period—rather the contrary.

The blind poet Antonio Feliciano de Castilho (born in 1800) lives by virtue of the purity, perfection, and beauty of his style, though he is overshadowed not only by his predecessor, but by his immediate successor in point of time, the prose historian Alexandre Herculano, who achieved real greatness not so much by his artistry but by a biblical nobility, an almost hypnotic conviction and sincerity which is only to be found rarely in literature: it occurs in Herrera's *Odes on the Battles of Lepanto and Alcacer Kibir*, in Cervantes' verse-play the *Siege of Numancia* (of which Shelley said if this was not poetry, he could not imagine a better substitute for it), in Prudentius, and in passages of Lucretius. We might call his big Odes historico-religious sermons, but he grips one without tiring one, as Hugo does when he does the same thing. His two greatest poems are *A Cruz Mutilada* and *A Tempestade*.

After him comes the romantic poet Soases de Passos, who wrote a fine long religious poem *O Firmamento*, which reminds one of Espronceda's *Ode to the Sun*, but is rather a paean to its Creator than to the subject of the poem.

After the romantics we come to a Pleiad, known as the Coimbra group, largely because the chief poets in it were contemporaries as students there. But there is one outstanding and radiant contemporary figure, who, though bound to them by friendship, could not be relegated to any school, locality, or period—that is the exuberant, divinely happy, and delightful João de Deus, who was born in the 'deep south' of the Algarve, and sings as naturally as a cicada in a green pine, uniting the golden age to that of the *trovadores*, and both with our own. His poetry is more difficult to translate than that of any other Portuguese poet, because rapture cannot easily be transferred from one language to another. The glow vanishes. Poetry travels more easily in the ice of sorrow and despair.

The tortured and very great figure of Antero de Quental towers above the rest of his time (if we except the unclassifiable João de Deus) as the most considerable since Camões. He hailed from the Azores, and was a philosopher whose earnest and sincere search for a faith ended in despair and suicide, on finding he could not accept one.

His friend and contemporary, Guerra Junqueiro, not quite his equal, was a poet of a more combative type who wrote satires on *The Senility of God* and wasted much energy in political polemics, but wrote lyrics of a piercing poignancy, and robust poems in the Hugoesque vein. His skill in metre and sense of rhythm were of a consummate mastery. He died reconciled to the religion he had spent his life attacking.

We have translated here the *Hymn of the Morning* by Antero de Quental:

Hymn of the Morning

You rise, O chaste and happy light of day,
And grow, vibrating purely in the height,
To fill triumphant hearts, who yet can pray
Or hope, with rays immaculately bright!

But in my heart, the home of desolation,
You pour enormous grief: since it prefers
The pitchblack Night, stark twin of desperation,
Dense, solitary, still, where no sound stirs.

The dumb void, where no star is seen to peep,
Where no bird sings, nor whispering breezes blow,
And thought itself falls heavily asleep—
To this clear morning light, this blessed glow!

Because the Night's the image of Non-Essence,
The image of unaltering repose,
Of undisturbed oblivion and quiescence,
For which the world yearns, weary with its woes.

For fixed and drowned in it, the darkness stores
The universal nothingness of thought,
And scorns this tortured world, which it ignores
As one already dead, and come to naught.

Intrepidly interrogating Doom,
Which, like a traitorous felon, it arraigns,
It turns once more toward the vacuous gloom,
Where, Godlike, grand, and peaceful, it remains—

Because the Night in truth's own image fashions
Itself, beyond our transitory range,
Hallucinating forms and fleeting passions,
Where only fraud and sorrow never change.

But you, O glorious light, so clear and fresh,
What do you symbolise, save the deceit
That in its myriad and mysterious mesh
Involves the world, as in a winding-sheet.

What do you stand for? Universal treason
And promises renewed to our confusion;
Still to be perjured in and out of season!
Mother of Life you are—and of Illusion!

Others stretch out their hands to you and pray,
With faith and hope, for what they never gain.
Others their wealth and confidence will lay
On promises, and days that dawn in vain.

I? No! On seeing you, I ask 'What sorrow
And what new torture yet unproven, say,
Will now be taught me by the breaking morrow?'
I ask, 'Why has it dawned another day?'

Of old you were not there, most lovely Light.
You had no being. The Universe, unwist,
Lay sunk inertly in the boundless night
Of possibility, a doubtful mist.

What do you bring with every dawn, save only
This feeling and this consciousness of ours
Of cureless, endless impotence, and lonely,
Insatiable hunger that devours?

Of what are made the loveliest of our morrows?
Of battles, lamentations, groans, and terrors!
Of what are made our days? Of countless sorrows,
Miseries, chagrins, agonies and errors!

The sun, a ruthless sower, without stop,
Tirelessly runs through space, and here and there
Out of his lap showers forth his fatal crop,
The innumerable harvest of despair.

See how that cursèd cornland swells and heaves
In the hot light, and how it shakes with fear
Before the winds of life! Hark how it grieves
In endless sighs, monotonous and drear!

Now, spread in rich voluptuous waves at length,
It grows with fierce fecundity, and breeds
With the same subtle and tenacious strength
That is invincible in noxious weeds.

From ancient filth its vigour is absorbèd.
It feeds on putrefaction in the mire.
A fragrance that is moribund and morbid
Seems from its poisoned sap-veins to perspire.

Composed of charms both hazy and magnetic,
Within this langorous aroma furled
Of carnal ardour and of charm poetic,
Was born the poison that infects the world.

Now like a trumpet-peal through hills and valleys,
The placid morning wakes, and drives to war
The miseries of earth. Their hosts she rallies
Horribly clamouring from shore to shore.

Grim, sightless, furious, famine-stricken, see!
They rush to arms, exchanging blow for blow
In brutal, endless strife, where all must be
Vanquished forever. But extinguished? No!

Though, at this hour, they raise new arms and shields,
In the bright morning, swelled with brutish force,
And seek the direst proofs that battle yields,
Gay, cruel, reckless, and without remorse—

Nightfall will see them trampled in the mud
And bleeding, as they vainly try to spew
At Heaven, through a gargled froth of blood,
The last foul imprecation that they knew.

How many, too, the night will overtake,
Lone and forgot, though still upon their feet,
And weeping, as they lean upon a stake,
Dumb tears of those who recognise defeat!

And why and wherefore do you call them, Light,
(Inexorable Light, serene and cruel!)
To this uncertain life and ruthless fight,
With your false visions firing them like fuel?—

Like toys within the playful hand of Doom
With which to while a fleeting day of mirth,
Or will-o-wisps that flicker, fade, and fume
Between the agonies of death and birth . . .

They seem, within the tedious firmament,
Blasted by evil stars with cheating light,
Like bands of piteous spectres that lament
Or shadows following a dream in flight.

Ah, no! Most glorious and triumphant whiteness,
Take off from me the glamour and the rays
Of your great mantle of deluding brightness!
For to the sad and vacillating gaze

Of my tired eyes—all tarnished, dim and sick,
And bitter to my heart, appears the Day—
Like a forgotten torch whose dying wick
Lights up a monstrous charnel with its ray.

In vain with glory all around you ring me.
In vain you pierce me with a loving thrill.
You cause me fear. Horror is what you bring me!
I cannot love you, and I never will.

Symbolic of the Universal Guile,
The false appearances of fleeting shades,
Which Everlasting Evil, with a smile,
Disguises ere the swift perspective fades.

Symbol of Fraud! Out of the endless night
You made the Cosmos rise, already versed
In grief and evil, treachery and spite.
Symbol of all Existence! Be accurst!

And here follows, after this black thunderstorm of grief, the
translation of a poem which is filled with the calm, quiet light,
which he sought so vainly through his life, but with which he
could fill many pages. The whole poem is suffused with the
gentle and noble nature that made Antero so beloved during his
life by all who knew him.

The Most Holy Virgin
Full of Grace, Mother of Misericord

In a dream made of all that is uncertain,
Through long, unbroken hours of nightly pain,
I saw her pitying gaze, as through a curtain,
Where (more than pity) sorrow, too, was plain.

'Twas not the vulgar blaze of beauty's face,
Nor banal ardour that in youth we feel.
It was another light, another grace . . .
I know not even if it can be real. . . .

A mystic suffering, which chanced to render
All pardon in its gaze, with all that's tender,
And peaceful as the hour when we expire.

O vision, sad and pitiful! Still keeping
This silence, stay with me. Remain, thus weeping;
And let me dream my life away entire.

Gomes Leal, born in 1848, was more naturally lyrical than Guerra Junqueiro, but lacked his intellectual discipline and powers of co-ordination. He began, like his contemporaries, by writing the sort of sociological poetry that was written in England in the 'thirties, before the war 'called the bluff'. But it was through his later lyrical verse that he exerted the greatest influence on his contemporaries. He was a symbolist before his time, exploring, like Baudelaire, but independently of him, the *correspondences* of *Colour and Sound* (*Cor e Som* is one of his titles). The music of his verse is impeccable and his best work is to be found in *As Claridades do Sul*, *A Mulher de Luto* and *A História de Jesus*. João Penha, Gonçalves Crespo, Antonio Feijó, Conde de Monsaraz, Coelho de Carvalho were all good poets of Parnassian leanings both in form and subject.

This brings us to the first of the moderns, Cesário Verde, who wrote of the streets and the docks in traditional metres, but strictly eschewing all 'poetical' verbiage. His strength is chiefly in description, naturalistic and realistic, and he influenced most of the moderns of today. António Nobre is generally classed with him as the forerunner of the moderns. Camilo Pessanha, Eugénio de Castro, Augusto Gil, Afonso Lopes Vieira, Ângelo de Lima, Afonso Duarte, Mário Beirião, Florbela Espanca, Cabral do Nascimento, José Régio, Vitorino Nemésio, António Botto, Pedro Homem de Melo, Francisco Bugalho, Carlos Queiroz, Alberto de Serpa, Miguel Torga (also a short-story writer),

Casais Monteiro, and, the most important of them all, Teixeira de Pascoais, must all be mentioned in any survey. The most brilliant of the younger poets, Alberto de Lacerda, has already found a worthy English translator for *Seventy Seven Poems* by him, in the veteran translator and poet Arthur Waley. He is therefore well known to the English public.

We shall have to give that amazing poet Fernando Pessoa (1892–1935) a space to himself. He projected himself into four different poets each, writing with a completely different style of his own, and so real did their personalities become that in the end there was a vast correspondence between them, written by their progenitor, from all of them to each other. He was reared and educated in South Africa at the Durban High School, so he started writing in English and published two books, one longish poem called *Antinous*, which is good, and a book of Sonnets, which are very bad, except that they become excellent the minute they are translated into Portuguese. His English prose was masterly, and equal in subtlety, delicacy, and accuracy to that of any living English master. His book of sea poems, *Mensagem*, is a pæan to the maritime history of Portugal comparable in that respect to nothing since the *Lusiads*. In fact many moderns rank Pessoa as second only to Camões in Portuguese poetry.

Of his pseudo-selves, Álvaro de Campos, a first engineer on a tanker, who wears a monocle and is of Jewish extraction, as Pessoa was himself, was in his poetry a thundering great extrovert crossed between Marinetti and Whitman. *The Maritime Ode* is the loudest poem ever written. For a hundred pages it is a series of deafening foghorn blasts, except for a quieter passage which I have translated here. Pessoa's other two pseudonyms were Alberto Caeiro (a very quiet and sincere poet of the countryside) and Ricardo Reis, a slightly morose, neo-pagan, but fine classical poet. Both these latter left good-sized volumes, but less than their mental progenitor, who was outwritten in bulk by Álvaro de Campos, whom he seems to have fancied more than his other mental offspring.

Pessoa, as a man, was a shadowy, retiring person: my elder

brothers were at school in Durban with him, but scarcely remember him, though his closest school friend, my friend, Mr. Ormond, corresponded with him for twenty years and seems to have been the only person ever to have got to know him. His literary friends in Lisbon speak of him as of a ghost: and Dr. Gaspar Simões, in his monumental book on his life and work, though he knew him personally, says it was harder to find particulars of his life than of anyone else's who had died 200 years ago. It is strange that a person whose name, Pessoa, *means* 'person', should be at the same time so impersonal, and yet able to project such thundering personalities as Álvaro de Campos, whose character is so real that you have to pinch yourself while reading him to remind yourself that this amazing spouter of blood and thunder is fictitious. Some of the best poetry of Pessoa, in his own name, often trembles on the very verge of silence, like Verlaine's. Here are three little poems from Pessoa himself, followed by a passage from the *Maritime Ode* by way of contrast between the miniaturist and his megalomaniac pseudonym, Álvaro de Campos, whose maritime poems are very different from the superbly controlled yet powerful poems in *Mensagem*.

FERNANDO PESSOA

Poem

The thing that hurts and wrings
Was never in my heart.
It's one of those fair things
In life that have no part.

Shapes without shape—each shade
Seems silently to flit
Ere known by grief, and fade
Ere love can dream of it.

They are as if our grief
Were a dark tree from whom
They flutter leaf by leaf
Into the mist and gloom.

Another

Death comes before its time,
Life is so brief a stay.
Each moment is the mime
Of what is lost for aye.

Life scarcely had begun,
Nor the idea diminished,
When he whose task was done
Knew not what he had finished.

This, doubting Death presumes
To cancel and to cut
Out of the book of dooms,
Which God forgot to shut.

Another

The poet fancying each belief
So wholly through and through
Ends by imagining the grief
He really feels is true.

And those who read what he has spelt
In the read grief feel good—
Not in the two griefs he has felt,
But one they never could.

Thus to beguile and entertain
The reason, does he start,
Upon its rails, the clockwork train
That's also called the heart.

From the *Maritime Ode* (Álvaro de Campos)

The whole quay is a memory in stone.
And when the ship leaves it, and suddenly
One sees the space widen
Between the quay and the ship,

I feel, I know not why, a recent anguish,
A haze of mournful feeling,
That shines in the sun of my grief
Like the first pane on which the morning shimmers.
It clothes me in the memory of another being
Whose person was mysteriously mine.

Who knows? Who knows if I have never
Embarked, before myself, from such a quay?
As a ship in the oblique rays of the morning sun, who knows
If I have not sailed from a different kind of port?
Who knows if I have not left (before the time
Of this exterior world as I behold it
Striping itself with colours for my sake)
A great Quay filled with the fewness of the people
Of as vast, as distended and apoplectic a city
As can exist outside of Space and Time.

Yes . . . from a quay in some way material,
Visible as a quay, real, and truly a quay,
The Absolute Quay, from whose model, unconsciously were copied,
And insensibly evoked,
All the quays of our ports,
Our quays of actual stone in actual water,
Which, once constructed, announce themselves
As Real-Things, Spirit-Things, or Entities of the Stone-Soul,
Made ours at certain moments by root-sensations,
When in the outer world, as if a door were opened,
But altering nothing,
The All in its diversity is shown.

Ah, the great quay from which we sailed as Nation Ships!
The great Anterior Quay, eternal and divine!
From what port? In what waters? (Or else, how could I think it?)
A great Quay, like the others, but uniquely THE Quay,
Filled, like the rest, with rustling silences before the dawn,
And unwinding at daybreak in a roar of cranes and winches,
With trains arriving full of merchandise
Under the occasional, light cloud

Of smoke from nearby factories,
Which shadows its floor
Black with sequinned atoms that twinkle
As if it were the shade of a dark cloud
Passing over the face of black water.

And here, to end up, are two translations to illustrate two very
desperate tendencies in modern Portuguese verse, the sophisticated bucolic and the modern pessimo-optimistic.

Irrigation (Francisco Bugalho)

Slow, far, and melancholic,
With old songs still renewed,
The water-wheel goes round.
The breezes blow bucolic
(Lyrical solitude!)
And make my doors resound.

The thirsty air awaits
Yearningly all the day
Till afternoon returns,
And now the strain abates.
The kiss of the sun's ray
Warms, but no longer burns.

In fragrance all things fume,
To all who breathe, recalling
Some sensual indiscretion.
The fireflies light the gloom,
And moist, warm Earth seems falling
For masculine possession.

The waterwheel is hushed,
But murmuring onwards still,
Through ruts and rills afar,
In light, soft whispers rushed,
Reflecting water thrills
To each unfeeling star.

Here is what I call the pessimo-optimistic—by that powerful poet José Regio, who is here making the best of a bad job with a vengeance.

Fado-Canção

I meditate my own strange lot.
I sing, and know the reason for it.
I sing because I have no better
Gift than this of song.
I sing to fortify myself
Against the silence, and the emptiness
Of my frustrated life,
Against the chill
Which percolates my being—
Like someone who, when night has fallen,
Has got to pass the cross-roads,
And lifts his trembling voice in song
To drive away his terror . . .
Behind the melody,
Which almost seems to speak,
A tragic statue stands in silence.
But sweet the rhythm is that lulls one,
And sweet the rhyme that lures one on,
And so I sing because it eases me
To listen to myself, although
The statue, as in granite, stands
Fixing its eyes afar,
And lifts a finger to its lips
Which stifles and prevents,
Upon those lips that frame a cry,
The cry from being uttered . . .

I also sing because I know
My song does not express me.
No one will ever find more in it
Than play of rhyme or rhythm.
I know quite well, that right up there,
And right down here below
I suffer all alone, hovering in silence—

L

But yet I sing, to leave
An echo thrilling in the air
Of the futile lullaby
That the sleeping world enjoys.

Ah! There are things that few men know!
But I know
So profoundly!
Those few men, yes, perhaps, may know them,
But cannot feel them truly.
I sing them, and its plain
That none can recognise them
In the alien tone I give them.
I can never arrive in their midst,
Even when it appears
That, escaping from my own enchantment,
I find myself with my own set of people.
I know all that—I know it well.
I know much more—But still, I sing.

Yes, I sing.
It is my destiny.
But I sing as a child screams
Who clings to the balcony
Of a building that's on fire,
In which he is left forgotten . . .
The square, beneath, is empty.
The sky, above, is hidden.
The balcony is dizzily high;
The ladders are turned to dust and ashes.
The crazy floor is crumbling.
The scream of anguish alone
Pierces an echo in the distance . . .
And no-one comes to his rescue.

I know that no-one is coming,
No-one at all.
The solitude, of which I'm dying,
Lends me a helping hand,

And exchanges a look of kindness
Which saves me from my panic . . .
But how much the better I know
And how much more devoutly believe in
That echo that sounds in the distance . . .

So the louder and better I sing!

CHAPTER EIGHT

Portuguese Prose

PORTUGUESE CULTURE, literature, and art have been firmly rooted, from the earliest times, in the Christian faith. It is not a surface culture, as ours is outside Britain. If you speak to Swazis, or Basutos on British territory, you have almost invariably to address them in their own languages. If you ask them their race, they will say, 'African'. But ask a Goanese, or Angolan negro, or a native of Timor what his race is: the last thing they dream of replying is 'Indian', 'African', or 'Polynesian': the proud answer you get from them all is, 'We are Portuguese.' When the Dutch, French, and English were jointly attacking the vast Portuguese Empire which stretched from the uncharted sources of the Amazon to the uttermost ends of Cathay and Polynesia, they had to speak Portuguese to establish any contact or understanding with the natives. The earliest Portuguese prose (in Latin) dates from the Arian–Priscillan contentions in the fourth century, while Portugal was yet Lusitania. In these contentions Bishops Potamio and Itatio, of Olissipo and Ossonoba [1] respectively, played a prominent part, and their thundering polemics rocked the length and breadth of Europe. Braga then became a centre of culture with the learned writing of St. Martin of Dume, St. Frutuoso, and Paulo Osorio, the emulous follower of St. Augustine in his Christian interpretation of Universal History.

In the latter half of the twelfth century was born Portugal's greatest gift to humanity, St. Anthony 'of Padua', as he became in the last ten years of his life, though for the first twenty-five he was really 'of Lisbon', where he was born, bred, and educated.

[1] Lisbon and Faro.

He left several immortal sermons which are of divine inspiration, though sometimes they breathe the more earthly fire with which he lashed the heresies of the age. A Doctor of the Church, and a 'highbrow', who has had more literature written about him of recent years than any saint except St. Francis himself, his discourses are on a lofty intellectual plane. Yet amongst the 'lowbrow' peasants of Portugal and Spain no other saint is so beloved. His youthful image, in almost every church, has none of the austere severity of some other saints, and he is revered and loved as a producer of husbands for plain spinsters and an almost infallible restorer of lost property. He died in 1231 in Padua, where he is still as beloved as when the Paduans would close their shops to hear his sermons, and the women sat all night in church to keep their seats.

A short while after St. Anthony of Lisbon, the Portuguese Pope John XXI—in other words, Petrus Hispanus, as he was before he became Pope—wrote the famous *Summulae Logicales*, which until 1550 or thereabouts was used in all the universities of Europe as the standard work for the study of Logic. He also wrote two famous treatises, *De Anima* and *Thesaurus Pauperum*, amongst numerous other philosophical and even medical works.

In a more pertinent setting, in relation to horsemanship, I referred to the two earliest secular works of Portuguese prose, that on hunting by King Dom João the First, and that on equitation by King Dom Duarte, who also wrote another famous work, *The Book of Loyal Counsel*. Prince Pedro, translator of Seneca, also wrote *The Book of Virtuous Bounty* (1392–1449). These prose works, in violent contrast to Portuguese poetry, have none of the lyricism of the latter, but remind one of the robust and sturdy realism of St. Thomas More. Aubrey Bell goes so far as to ascribe this outstanding quality of strict, objective realism 'literary but not lyrical' to the English blood in the veins of the royal house of Aviz! But it constitutes the very nature of Portuguese prose down to the present day. Nowhere is that quality more clearly to be found than in the Latin works of Petrus Hispanicus to which we have just referred, and those of Paulo

Osorio, neither of whom had a drop of English blood in his veins!

There are a few exceptions, but, generally speaking, it would seem that two distinct currents rush straight through Portuguese literature, from its beginnings to now, without blending, though parallel; the one lyrical, subjective, and emotional; and the other severe, objective, and intellectual. The two principles are complementary, the male and female of one race.

Fernão Lopes (1380–1450), for a mediæval chronicler, was in advance of contemporary chroniclers, and was already a true historian in the modern sense; he was not only a fascinating recorder, like Froissart, but, without such credulity, an indefatigable sifter and investigator of facts, and a sharp critic, with a full sense of all the political and social complexities of history, though this in no way detracted from his charm as a narrator. He may be said (in his *Cronicas* of King Ferdinand and King John 'of blessed memory') to be the first truly great Portuguese prose writer, if we discount the famous thirteenth-century *Amades de Gaula* of Vasco de Lobeira, which was lost, but has been retranslated back into Portuguese, in our times, by Afonso Lopes Vieira, from the Spanish translation of Montabo, done in 1508.

Another fine chronicler, chiefly for the deep feeling and drama of his tale, is Father João Álvares with his *Cronica do Infante Santo*, which inspired one of Calderon's greatest plays, *The Constant Prince*. This is the story of Prince Ferdinand's heroic life and death as a Christian martyr and a voluntary captive of the Moors, when he underwent torture and captivity rather than give back the captured city of Ceuta.

By the beginning of the sixteenth century the conquest of the great empire of Portuguese prose had begun, first by the didactic princes of Aviz, then by Vasco Lobeira with his lost *Amadis* (which, none the less, bore priceless fruit) and by Fernão Lopes. Other chroniclers at the end of the fifteenth century were Ruy de Pina and Gomes Eanes de Azurara.

Bernardim Ribeiro, the great poet, a sort of Cyrano, unlucky with women, who died at the battle of Alcacer Kibir, wrote the

Livro das Saüdades, a long love-poem in prose, in a pastoral style, and, with it, bucolicism was introduced into Portugal. Though uneven, the poem is full of piercing beauties, and succeeds where Cervantes in his *Galatea*, Sidney in his *Arcadia*, and Lyly in his *Euphues* all failed so completely. This is because Ribeiro's thwarted passion takes fire, thrills, and wrings us almost the whole time. Heine once described Berlioz as 'a skylark the size of an eagle'. Reading this prose-poem is like listening to *a nightingale the size of a man*. In fact the passage which the Portuguese love to quote most refers to a nightingale. English is not the best language in which to render the tender trills and moans to which the Portuguese and Italian languages can give utterance without sentimentality; but as this passage is the most famous in Portuguese prose, and, in the original, one of the most musically moving in literature, I risk the following translation so as to give the reader an idea of the theme:

While I was thus plunged in my reverie, it was not long before a nightingale came and sat on a green bough overhanging the waters. He began to sing in so sweet a voice that I was soon entirely taken up with listening to him. He redoubled his laments, till I thought he must cease from sheer fatigue, but he always began to sing more beautifully still. Then in the midst of his plaints, I know not how, he suddenly fell dead on the waters. As he fell between the boughs, many leaves fell with him and I took it as a sign of mourning and sympathy for so great a misfortune. He drew the ripples after him, and the leaves after the ripples. I should have loved to fetch him, but at that spot the currents are too swift, and the thickets on the water-edge too thorny; and soon he disappeared out of sight. My heart was so seized to see one, who had sung so sweetly a moment before, fall so suddenly dead, that I could not stop my tears.

A magnificent powerful prose comedy, *Eufrosina*, was written by Jorge Ferreira de Vasconcellos in about 1540, a rival to Lope's great prose drama *La Dorotea* and to the *Celestina* of Francisco de Rojas, one of the great landmarks of the Spanish drama, about which so many hundreds of books and treatises have been written. Yet, though quite as great, hardly anything has ever been written about the *Eufrosina*. These great plays all deal in a truly realistic way with the seamy side of life and give you Breughel-like pictures of Portuguese and Spanish life in, and *on*, the streets in the sixteenth century. They depict the worst type of procuresses and the havoc they can work. You come across the same types in Cervantes' *Entremeses*.

Though such powerful realistic dramas co-existed with the chivalresque novels (as *Bartholomew Fair* and *Arden of Feversham* did with the *Arcadia* and *Euphues* in England) in Portugal, it was the latter that were the dominant influence. Amadis and his progeny of Clarimonds and Palmerins almost entirely held the imagination of the people of Portugal and Spain at a time when a race of heroes was setting off, every week, into the unknown, on expeditions as fabulous and fantastic as anything ever undertaken by Amadis, Palmerin, or Orlando Furioso; for, to them, it was quite possible, in those days, that if they sailed far enough, they would fall off the edge of the world or reach the rising sun or setting moon. As Amadis preceded, and Clarimond and Palmerin coincided, with the start of all this world-errantry, it is quite possible to say that they *caused*, rather than merely *stimulated*, these quests, which ended in Japan, Tibet, Central China, Abyssinia, Australasia, Mexico, the Andes, Labrador, and the Cape: quests so unbelievable that the most exact cartographers and the most accurate narrators (like Mendes Pinto) could be dismissed so much later as in the time of Johnson and Congreve in England as a shameless bunch of lying Munchausens and Mandevilles. It took the more recent Burtons, Livingstones, Bruces, etc., to confirm them to the English.

The two main offspring of their Portuguese ancestor *Amadis de Gaula* were naturally Portuguese. Even in the expert opinion of their great rival, Cervantes, who wrote three books of 'errantry' —the weak *Galatea*, the great *Don Quixote*, and the perhaps even greater *Persiles*—it is the authors of *Amadis* and *Palmerim*, the two Portuguese, who deserve the laurels, although Cervantes was superior to either, as Shakespeare is to Chaucer. The *Chronicle of the Emperor Clarimond*, a book of knight-errantry, was written in his youth by João de Barros (later to become the great historian) for the amusement, and perhaps the chivalrous formation, of the young Prince João, to whom he was tutor. It appeared in the early sixteenth century. João de Barros later became one of the greatest of the many historians of the era of discoveries.

Next in importance and fame to *Amadis* itself, comes the *Chronicle of Palmerim of England* by Francisco de Morais. This latter, with *Amadis de Gaula*, is one of the few volumes in Don Quixote's library that, in Chapter VI of the First Part, are not given by the Parish Priest and the Barber (Don Quixote's friends) to the housekeeper to be burned; and the following dialogue shows the truly great respect and love that the greatest master of his time (the generation preceding Shakespeare's) in any country, Cervantes, had for these books by Portuguese masters:

The first book that Maese Nicolas handed to him was *Amadis de Gaula*, and the priest said:

'That is a mysterious coincidence, since from all I've heard, it was the first book of "errantry" to be printed in Spain; and as it is the origin of all the others, it appears to me that, as the dogmatiser of the whole heresy, without any excuse, it should be the first to be condemned to the fire.'

'No, your reverence,' said the barber, 'because I have heard it said that it is by far the best of all books of this kind: and as the unique of its kind, it should be spared.'

The next book *Sergas de Esplandian* (also of Portuguese origin) gets short shrift:

'Sergas,' said the Barber, 'is the legitimate son of *Amadis*.'

'Well,' said the good priest, 'the son cannot expect to profit by the goodness of his father. Take it from him, Madam Housekeeper: open that window: and throw it into the corral as the beginning of the heap for the bonfire.'

There is quite a big heap by the time the Priest and the Barber come upon *Palmerim of Oliva* along with *Palmerim of England*.

Hereupon the Priest puns on the olive and the palm suggested by the titles:

'As for that *Olive*,' said the priest, 'you can cut it up and burn it, till not a cinder remains; but as for that *Palm* of England, let it be preserved in a special box of its own, like that priceless casket which Alexander selected from the spoils of Darius to contain his copy of Homer. This book, Señor my friend, has authority for two reasons: firstly because it is so good; and secondly because it is said to have been written by a most wise King (*sic*) of Portugal. All the adventures of the Castle of Miraguardas are most excellent, and of the greatest art: the arguments are polished and clear, and suited to his subject with the greatest aptitude and the deepest knowledge. I therefore say, Señor Master Nicolas, that, saving your own good opinion, this book, together with *Amadis de Gaula*, remain free from the fire, and that without any more palavering, let the whole of the rest of the library perish!'

We have seen how these two books, and the torrent of imitations which they generated, stimulated, if they did not cause, the discovery of New Worlds in the east and west. But we owe them more lasting achievements than that in the world of letters, not only in themselves, as great works of art, towering above the cardboard imitations of Sidney's *Arcadia* and Lyly's *Euphues*, which, themselves, exerted a tremendous influence on our Elizabethans: but in the great books, their descendants, that could not have been written without them. All authors whose heroes go on journeys—not for a set *material* purpose like Jason for the fleece, like Ulysses, who was trying to get home, or Æneas, who was fleeing for his life—but in search of trouble, adventure, fun, or salvation, are sons of Vasco de Lobeiro, and their heroes are sons of *Amadis de Gaula*. What a tremendous literature grew from this one book! *Orlando Furioso*, *Morte d'Arthur*, the superb *Comedias Novelescas* of Calderon, *Pantagruel*, *Don Quixote*, *Persiles*, *The Faery Queen*, *Pilgrim's Progress*, *Hudibras*, *Giarusaleme Liberata*, *The Lusiads* (in great part)—one could fill a page with them, as one could with their flesh-and-blood brothers, equally the sons of Amadis, seekers of adventure, who set off 'into the blue' without knowing exactly where—Columbus, da Gama, Bartolomeo Diaz, Velho Cabral, Gil Eannes, Labrador, Cortes, Tristan da Cunha, Pizarro, Ercilla, Camões, Lancarota, Alvares Cabral, Magellan, and his second-in-command, the Spaniard, who (*not* Magellan [1]) was the first to sail round the world—Sebastian el Cano, who navigated the least-known waters, and bore the brunt. Tschiffely, the lone horseman of the 'Rides', in modern times, was the last of this great brotherhood, descended via Don Quixote (his favourite reading), from the original Portuguese Amadis. Like Camões, Cervantes, and Ercilla, so often depicted with a sword in one hand and a pen in the other, he was as fine a writer as a man of action, the last of such people we shall ever see, perhaps, in a world of specialists.

Paradoxically enough, it was not only geographical discovery that was heralded by this old-fashioned form of literature, the *novela caballerisca*. What is the flying castle of Lindabridis but a dirigible zeppelin, or a big modern airliner, in embryo? Orlando's trip to the moon is now a possibility and will soon be a reality.

At the same period of the early and middle sixteenth century, other Portuguese writers were 'discovering' Europe: Francisco de Holanda, friend of the Lady Vittoria Colonna, Michelangelo, and Cellini, wrote a treatise on the painters of antiquity. Gonçalo Fernando Trancoso made an inventory of the national wealth of

---

[1] Magellan perished at the Philippines before he got halfway round. They were Spanish ships and it was a Spanish expedition, with all-Spanish crews. English history has been singularly mean and dishonest about Spanish marine prowess, even to suppressing the last round of the Armadas, in which Drake, Hawkins, Raleigh, Cobham Brooke, were so thunderingly hounded off the Spanish Main by Avellanada at the Antilles and elsewhere. Drake died of shock and diarrhoea after the battle.

The Spaniards make no secret of their defeat at Trafalgar; and the way they invited the English wounded ashore, and nursed them with their own, was an example to the world. If Gravina, who had twice worsted Nelson (you can see the Union Jacks at Teneriffe and Cartagena) had been allowed to command instead of Villeneuve, the results might have differed. He disagreed and wished to attack first as Nelson did. But they both died in the same battle.

his own native country in popular fables and folk-tales, adding some of his own, of which he compiled the equivalent of the *Contes de Perrault* or *Grimms' Fairy Tales*, entitled *Contos e Historias de Proveito e Exemplo* (*Exemplary and Edifying Tales*). To this day traditional stories which have been handed down orally, whether included in his collection or not, are known as 'Tales of Trancoso'.

A Portuguese of Goa (what *we* would call an Indian, but few Goanese will not flare up at that) wrote a book mostly in prose, partly in verse, on the Italian model, under the title of *Lusitania Transformada*, of which half the scene is laid in Portugal and half in India, thus introducing the Indian landscape as an entirely new feature in pastoral poetry, but not so awkwardly as our Bishop Heber in his love-poem from India to his wife.

The Iberian Empires, not being commercial, like the British and Dutch Empires, produced great literatures at once. Our colonial literature is still a mere fœtus after our whole Empire has collapsed. The Australians claim English-born poets, like Adam Lindsay Gordon, as theirs. Camões, at that rate, is a colonial poet. He was an exile, a convict of the 'Botany Bay' type, exiled for striking one of the King's guard with his sword. If we compare Adam Lindsay Gordon to Camões, we get a proportionate idea of our colonial literature in comparison either to the Portuguese or to Spanish, which can also claim an epic nearly as great as *The Lusiads*—personally, I prefer the *Araucana* (much as I love *The Lusiads*) simply as I prefer steel (which I know how to handle in many forms) to silver and gold, for that is how they compare, and my preference is merely a personal idiosyncrasy. But the *Araucana* derives from *The Lusiads*. My critical sense tells me I am wrong, and I know it. This brings us to the great prose work of Camões. This was called his *Treasury*, and in it he stored all the treasures of his thought—philosophical, critical, philological, religious, reflective, or reminiscent. It was stolen from his haversack in Moçambique, when he was on his way home to get it published. This was a far greater loss to Portuguese literature than the original of *Amadis*—since at least that exists in translation. But the *Treasury*, like Sappho's poems and Sylla's memoirs, is lost for ever.

Portugal had become the centre of the world for all those for whom the science of the old classical doctors could no longer suffice. The foremost among those who came to wonder, to study, to learn, and to write, was Christopher Columbus himself, who wrote as well, if not as much, in Portuguese as in Spanish.

Before Bacon, the Portuguese were the first to study nature by proof and trial, rather than from the texts of the ancients. In 1537 Pedro Nunes, in his treatise on the Globe and in his *De Crepuscules*, explained, in the most beautiful language reminiscent of Lucretius, the reasons for the differences in the durations of twilights and sunsets on different parts of the earth. Astro-navigation, still used, apparently, in modern aviation,[1] and known to the ancients, whether for bush, desert, or sea navigation, was first re-discovered in Portugal, where the quadrant was also invented. In loxodromy Portugal was ahead of every other race. One of the most fascinating things that ever came my way was to be able to study the notes made by Columbus in his own handwriting in Portuguese and Spanish in the margins of books by Pope Pius II and Pierre d'Ailly, where it is said that the Torrid Zone is uninhabitable and where he corrects other misconceptions. His prose is always magnificent, biblical, prophetic, and rabbinical, pointing obviously, as his best biographer, Dr. Madariaga, states, to his Hebrew origin. The best is to be found in his Spanish letters to the Catholic Kings. But here is an enchanting note he wrote in the margin of the *Imago Mundi* while he was serving his ten years' apprenticeship on Portuguese ships, and at Henry the Navigator's observatory down at Sagres, near Cape St. Vincent— a weighty fragment which should not be omitted from any prose anthology: 'The Torrid Zone is not *uninhabitable*, for the Portuguese are sailing to and fro in it today. On the very Equator

---

[1] Flying over the Sahara, the South African air hostess took me into the holy of holies where the pilots functioned, and showed me the glass dome through which they were guiding their aptly-named 'Constellation', by the rules of Henry the Navigator!

itself stands the castle of Mina belonging to His Most Serene Majesty, the King of Portugal, which we have seen.'

You can picnic among the ruins of this observatory, which was destroyed by an earthquake. There, sitting with a sprig of rosemary forked through a newly-roasted kebab of lamb (or a fresh tunny-steak) in one hand and a leather bottle of good red wine in the other, and a fragrant fire of wild thyme smouldering at your feet, with Trafalgar on your left and St. Vincent on your right, gaze out over the spray-thundering cliffs across the Atlantic, as Columbus must have done during his studies, at lunch break. I defy you to repeat, in that enchanted spot, those few words in Portuguese or English (as I once did, not even explaining to my guests either the authorship or the context) without sending a shiver up your own spine and those of your companions. Looking straight out to Tristan da Cunha and the Americas, we all suddenly forgot our food and drink, and even each other, and stood up and looked over the sea (landsmen and all!), each one of us seemingly possessed by the ghosts of those who did so centuries before us, each one of us alone with himself:

> Like a lone sentry with a piercing view,
> Who keeps his watch on the Leucadian height
> And sees the vessels ere they heave in sight
> With forms that faintly tremble in the blue.
>   *Baudelaire*

That paragraph of prose by Columbus has the explosive power of the 'mighty atom'—it is like a verse from the Psalms. The mighty intellect and heart that hatched both Americas out of the blue, can make two plain little sentences outweigh all the ponderous tomes of that frost-bitten minotaur of frigid circumlocutions to whom sentences were labyrinths—Henry James! [1]

[1] The coast round here is haunted by even older memories than that of Columbus or the Navigator. Cape St. Vincent, beyond Sagres, is famous for its sunsets, which are often magnified out of all proportion by the strange atmospherics. It was venerated as the "*Sacred Promontory*" by Romans, Greeks, Phœnicians, and Lusitanians alike. Here you can sometimes see the phenomenon of "the green flash", so common near the equator, as the last

In the same spirit of scientific inquiry, with a Latin title but a Portuguese text, the great cartographer Duarte Pacheco wrote his *Esmeraldo de Situ Orbis*, an objective description of the African coast so minute and exact that it mentions small landmarks that we used to use on the Durban whale-chasers in the old days, before the mother-ships and floating factories came into being—landmarks that you can only see at less than a mile from the shore. He knew, too, things about the Moçambique current and counter-current which local whalers and fishermen only found out recently. Apparently the Portuguese have known them all along. But if you are a simpleton enough ever to ask a fisherman: 'Where did you make that fine haul?' he will always point in the opposite, or the wrong, direction. The Basques were hunting sperm whales with hand-harpoons in the South Atlantic and Indian oceans long before Vasco da Gama was ever heard of. Portuguese Basque and Celtic fishermen were visiting the Newfoundland Banks at an early date, and must have known of the existence of land there, though they took no interest in it. Even to this day the Portuguese hardly ever land, though they have an ambulance launch that cruises between the cod-fleet and Halifax. Kipling gives a fine account of the cod-fleet in *Captains Courageous*, and Alan Villiers, who made the trip, won the Camões prize with an even finer account. Celtiberian fishermen either settled in America or were shipwrecked there before Leif Ericson discovered America, since the Celts gave up the general use of coracles before that date. Yet in Catlin's account of the now extinct Mandan Indians, published in 1830, and in his pictures of them drawn on the spot, we find a considerable percentage of Gaelic words in their vocabulary, they have blue eyes, and they use coracles, made of skins and withies, instead of the more practical birch-bark canoes. They also had Welsh cradles (instead

point of a vastly magnified sun vanishes in the sea. They used to say you could hear the hiss of the red-hot solar globe being quenched, at the same time in the waves. The far-down hiss of the waves, coming up from the cloven cliffs and the holes at their base, is at moments realistic enough to account for the belief.

of papoose slings) of exactly the same model as the carpenter at Aberdaron made for my child born there in 1922. I have seen these cradles too in the north of Portugal, where Celtic survivals seem to endure longest, presided over by the Colossus of Pedralva, one of the most imposing idols ever carved in stone, looking like a monstrous edition of that great Celt, Augustus John, in his bath. That America should have been 'discovered' by the hunger and dire necessity of fishermen centuries before its public scientific discovery is well in keeping with the general 'cageyness' of fishermen. Having been both a whaler and a professional tunny-fisher, the greatest difficulty I had in writing this book was in disclosing good places to fish in. I can easily believe that Labrador made his find through a cod-fisherman getting drunk and letting the cat out of the bag that there was 'land up there', after centuries of keeping the secrecy of the confessional itself, in their own self-interest, for the monopoly of cod, by generations on generations of fishermen.

The cunning, the hunger, the dire necessity or greed of the primitive hunter is always first on the spot, and it is quite feasible to imagine a posse of Esquimaux sitting round the carcass of a polar bear on the very North Pole itself, without being conscious of the fact, centuries before Peary had his photo taken with the Stars and Stripes flying over him. It is the conscious discoverer, however, who brings the poetry with him and miraculously transfigures what to the fishermen had been no more than dangerous lee-shores into the aviating, starry towers of Manhattan, or the hanging gardens of Rio, Durban, or Funchal.

Another, perhaps even greater, cartographer was D. João de Castro, who in his *Roteiros* gave the explanation of many till then unsolved phenomena, such as the deviations of the magnetic needle, and charted the Red Sea, the route from Lisbon to Goa, and from Goa to Suez.

A great prose work which was also another pre-Baconian labour of experimental science was published in Goa in 1553 by the botanist Garcia da Orta under the title of *Coloquio dos Simples e Drogas*. This is a revolutionary work which confounds the authority of the ancients by experiment and scientific investigation. It was the first work of *Modern Medicine*. Friar Tome de Jesus wrote *The Labours of Jesus* at about this time, a book of such great beauty that Aubrey Bell said it was worthy to rank as 'the Fifth Gospel'.

In 1735 there appeared in Lisbon a great classic—a collection of tales of this period, which is entirely unique of its kind in the whole world, and could only have been collected and edited in Portugal. This was the *Tragico-Maritime History*, consisting of the narratives of the survivors of all the most notable shipwrecks of the sixteenth and seventeenth centuries, whether written by the survivors or told by them orally and written down by various editors during those 200 years. Some of these are absolutely masterly stories—especially *The account of the very notorious loss of the great galleon the 'São João' (Saint John) in which are told the great hardships and misadventures of the captain*

MANUEL DE SOUSA SEPULVEDA

and the pitiful end to which he himself, his wife and children and nearly all the rest of his people came in the land of Natal where they were cast on the 24th of June 1552.

Next to the Episode of Inés de Castro (the mistress of King Pedro the Just, who was so cruelly murdered by his father, Alfonso IV), this episode has inspired more poetry than any other in Portuguese history, but even when Camões treats it in his best style, making it a part of the wild prophetic speech, with which the giant Adamastor, the horrific apparition of the Spirit of the Cape, tries to terrify the intrepid Vasco on his way round, it falls short of the poetical pathos of the original simple prose narrative, especially where the noble and beautiful Portuguese lady, stripped of her clothes by the kaffirs, digs herself deep into the beach sand to hide her nakedness from them—though they seem to have been singularly insensitive to European beauty in those days, since they offered her no other violence than robbery. Here in Fanshawe's quaint English is the passage from *Adamastor's* prophecy that was inspired by these twenty odd pages of

M

tragic prose I ever read. It gives the tragedy in a few
damastor is speaking:

Another shall come after, of good *fame*,
A *Knight*, a *Lover*, and a *lib'ral Hand*,
And with him bring a fair and gentle *dame*
Knit by his LOVE and HYMEN'S sacred Band.
In an ill hour, and to your loss and shame,
Ye come within the *Purlews* of my land;
Which (kindly cruel) from the *sea* shall free you,
Drowned in a *sea* of miseries to see you.

Starved shall they see to death their *Children* deare,
Begot, and rear'd, in so great love. The black
Rude CAFRES (out of *Avarice*) shall teare
The *Cloathes* from the *Angellick Lady's* back.
Her dainty limbs of *Alabaster* clear
To *Heate*, to *Cold*, to *Storm*, to *Eyes'* worse *Rack*
Shall be laid *naked*; after she hath trod
(Long time) with her soft Feet the burning Clod.

(Canto V: Stanzas 46–7)

I can remember as a small boy an Umkuthla tree in Cornubia
forest, a couple of miles north of the Umgeni mouth, which had a
galleon carved on the bark and some writing we could not de-
cipher. I used to go there as a boy to shoot buck and bushpig,
though it is now a flourishing suburb 'Durban North', and the
Umkuthla, or thunder-tree, probably six or seven hundred years
old, has been uprooted and destroyed. I have no doubt that the
galleon represented was the *São João*, since it was the only wreck
of any consequence on that coast till the nineteenth century. The
Birkenhead and the *Grosvenor* sank nearer the Cape, and were
frigates, not galleons. What confirms my belief is that between
the galleon and the undecipherable lettering was an arrow pointing north, the direction taken by the survivors. All other survivors of wrecks on that coast have always headed south. In the
Tragico-Maritime History there are several other narratives of
almost equal literary merit to the wreck of the *São João*. *The
wreck of the 'Santiago' in the year 1585 and the journeyings of those*

who were saved from it, was written by Manoel Godinho Cardoso and published in Lisbon in 1601. It ranks as truly great literature. This ship was wrecked much farther north on the same coast, and the adventures of the crew were more fabulous, if less tragic, than those of the crew of the *São João*. But the whole of the *Historia Tragico Maritimo* forms a national prose epic embodying so many acts of heroism, self-abnegation, daring, and devotion, that the horrors and sufferings depicted in almost every narrative are eclipsed by the shining and splendid heroism of the Portuguese sailors, from the humblest boatswains to the proudest admirals.

The greatest prose work of this period, and the prose rival of the *Lusiads* themselves, is the *Peregrination* of Fernão Mendes Pinto. For twenty-two years he wandered round the Far East as a soldier, pirate, merchant, ambassador, and admiral of corsairs. He was in the first ship to discover Japan. He met, and was so impressed by St. Francis Xavier, that he even took monastic vows and joined the Company of Jesus—from which he seems immediately to have been expelled! He returned to Portugal in the direst poverty, having squandered several fortunes and piles of ill-gotten treasure, but retaining the greatest of all treasures, his memory, from which he poured forth the wealth of his experience in the most vivid, natural, and vigorous prose. Living in poverty at Almada, relieved of his monastic vows, he married and had many children, for whose sake he wrote the story of his adventurous life 'thirteen times taken prisoner and seventeen times sold as a slave'. Almost all his descriptions of Central Asia, Peking, etc., have been checked as accurate by subsequent travellers and explorers; with the exception of the two episodes of the *Isle of Treasures* and the *Marvellous Island of Calampui*, which, *if* he was drawing on his imagination, then prove him to be quite as great a creative imaginist as he was a truthful narrator.

Diogo do Couto lived at Goa for fully fifty years of his life (1542–1616), as a soldier, official, merchant, and historian. He was a great friend of Camões. João de Barros, whom we have already mentioned, as the writer of *Clarimond*, the novel of

antry', had died in 1570, having become a great his-
bringing his chronicles *Décadas da Asia I, II, and III*
down to his own times. Diogo do Couto, the active eye-witness
of most of what he describes,[1] and the completely frank and fearless critic of some of his most exalted commanders-in-chief,
continued the *Décadas of Barros* from IV to XII. Philip II
appointed him the Grand Chronicler of the Indies, a title which
he would have earned anyway on his performance as a historian.
His great work, however, is the *Practical Soldier*, a book which
might be 'a pessimistic commentary on the *Lusiads*'—to quote
Osório de Oliveira.

A contemporary of his, the secretary of the greatest of the Vice-
Roys, Alfonso d'Albuquerque emulated Diogo worthily in his
Legends of India. The letters of Albuquerque himself to King
Manuel I are of prime importance as great prose: so are the
Commentaries of Afonso d'Albuquerque written by his son, Braz
d'Albuquerque. We must not forget either that prodigious,
saintly, and heroic missionary to the Moluccas, António Galvão,
with his extraordinary work *Treatise on the different routes by
which, in past times, pepper and spices came from the Indies to our
country, and also on all the Discoveries, ancient and modern, which
have been made up till the year 1550.*

The log of the caravel, São Rafael, kept by the first mate,
Alvaro Velho, serves as the Chronicle of Vasco da Gama's first
voyage to India. The prose is not elegant, but it is competent and
very memorable; and its title in Portuguese is *Roteiro da Viagem
que em descobrimento de India pelo Cabo de Boa Esperança fez
Dom Vasco da Gama.* This was the book from which the *Lusiads*
was written, except when it is autobiographical.

Other important works of travel at that period were the letter,
in 1500, of Pedro Vaz to King Dom John the Second, about the
discovery of Brazil; *The Lands of Prester John* being the narrative
of the Portuguese Embassy to Abyssinia; Padre Manoel
Godinho's *The Return from India*; and the *Voyage to Abyssinia*

---

[1] In our British literature the nearest thing we have to Diogo do Couto is
Napier's *Peninsula War*—if we cut out the strategical theorising.

(translated anonymously by Dr. Samuel Johnson, Birmingham 1735); *A Short Relation of the River Nilo* anonymous; and *A Historical Narrative of Abyssinia*. The last three are included in Dr. Charles David Ley's Everyman collection of *Portuguese Voyages* under the heading *The Jesuits in Abyssinia*. Francisco Rodrigues Lobo (1580–1622) wrote three Pastorals wherein verse alternates with prose, but he left a memorable work in *The Court of the Village and Winter Nights*.

The seventeenth century was the 'age of gold' for Portuguese prose, with Friar Luis de Sousa, Father António Vieira, Manuel Bernades, Friar Manuel de Melo, and Friar António das Chagas, who wrote the fiery and fervent *Spiritual Letters*. F. Luis de Sousa in his *Life of St. Dominic* and that of *Dom Frei Bartolomeu dos Martires* shows himself to be the finest stylist in the Portuguese language. He makes up in sheer writing for his obvious faults as a historian. Garrett, the leading romantic poet of the nineteenth century, wrote a popular tragedy about him, which keeps his memory fresh for the ordinary non-highbrow Portuguese public. But the masterly nineteenth-century prose writer, Camilo Castelo Branco, qualifies his life of the great Bishop as 'Divine'.

Father António Vieira whom the greatest of modern Portuguese poets, Pessoa, qualifies as the 'Emperor of our language' was, like Cicero or Bossuet, primarily an orator or a preacher, but, as in their cases, his eloquence remains in the written word. Senhor Osório de Oliveira says: 'Yes, he was the Emperor of our language, but not of our souls or our minds, because the first title belongs to Camões and the second to Francisco Manuel de Melo.'

Menendez y Pelayo, the most eminent scholar and critic of the last century, puts Francisco Manuel higher than any other prose-writer of the Peninsula, except Quevedo. Our own outstanding scholars Edgar Prestage and Aubrey Bell qualify him respectively as 'perhaps the greatest literary figure of the seventeenth century' and as a 'figure to whom no other Portuguese of the seventeenth century can be compared and very few of any period in the whole

he Peninsula.' He wrote a classic in Spanish, too, *The
War*. Then, at the age of forty, he wrote his *Letter of
Guidance to Married Couples* where he shows himself a writer of a
higher calibre, even as a moralist, more interesting, and more
modern than he is as a historian. His most vital works *The Guide
for Married Couples*, *Apologues in Dialogue* and *Familiar Letters*
are far more modern than Montaigne, and worthier to be the companions of the most up-to-date existentialist than the latest book
by Anouilh or Sartre. Most of these works were written in prison
or Brazilian exile, but with such a delightful serenity, that one
would think they were written on days of leisure, in summer. His
historical work written as a participant eye-witness of the destruction of the Portuguese Armada in France is described by Edgar
Prestage as an 'epic in prose'. He also wrote a comedy in con-
tinuation and modernization of Gil Vicente's *Auto do Fidalgo
Aprendiz* which the arch-thief Molière later stole for his *Bourgeois
Gentilhomme*. A book could be written, starting with this comedy,
to prove that the French dramatists, especially in their comedies,
depended entirely on Portuguese and Spanish drama. Molière
took *Don Juan*, *Le Bourgeois Gentilhomme*, *L'Amour Medecin*,
Tartuffe, *Le Misanthrope* and *Le Malade Imaginaire* straight from
vastly superior Portuguese and Spanish plays. What Racine
and Corneille did not pinch from Greek or Latin they took
from Portugal and Spain. Nobody who has read Tirso's *Don
Juan*, the profoundly spiritual, yet tragical and comical *Burlados
de Sevilla*, with its wonderful verbal description of Lisbon, as
detailed as Greco's half-map, half-landscape of Toledo, can ever
pick up and re-read Molière's cheap, tin-pot vulgarisation of that
supremely great play—on a level with Æschylus or Shakespeare.
Both Gil Vicente and Manuel de Melo are, similarly, far more pro-
found than the agile courtier poet of Louis XIV.

Father Manuel Bernardes did not resemble his great contemporaries of 'the age of gold' in Portuguese prose. He wrote in his
cell, from his heart. He was a verbal Fra Angelico. He is the
anti-stylist who takes the short cut every time, ambushing us with
simplicity, outflanking us with sincerity. He lacks all the orna-

ments of literature except vigour and directness, but he has enough of them to compensate the rest.

Not all the Religious, however, in Portugal were listening to the voices of seraphs and cherubim: *The Letters of a Portuguese Nun* (as passionate as those of Héloise) were written towards the end of the seventeenth century. Sister Mariana Alcoforado wrote with the passionate fury of a prose Sappho. It is said that these Portuguese Letters were 'touched-up' by French poets in Paris before publication in French; but the terrestrial love expressed therein is a credit either to the great-hearted love of Sister Mariana, or to the artistic skill of the 'touchers-up'.

We now reach the doldrums of Portuguese prose. With few exceptions hardly any good prose was written till *Journeys in my own Country*, by Almeida Garrett, the Romantic poet, who actually created modern Portuguese prose after a century or so of atrophy.

But the real master of prose in the Romantic period was the historian Alexandre Herculano, a 'liberal', but almost biblical figure, who was not only a great poet, but whose *History of Portugal* raised him head and shoulders above every other historian in a country where historians out-number and out-write every other kind of writer, having more motives and material for writing history than the writers of any other modern country.

An amazing writer followed Garrett and Herculano. It is rare to pass his statue in Lisbon without seeing it crowned or strewn with flowers. This is Camilo Castelo Branco (1825–90). He is not an artist, nor a writer, nor a poet—simply one of the greatest elemental forces that ever lived, a creature of prodigious humanity, passions, love, sarcasms, and hatreds. In the words of the critic Moniz Barreto:

In his hands, the novel renounces all its specific functions and transforms itself into elegy and satire. And it is in elegy and satire that he is triumphant. No other writer possesses to the same degree the gift of contagious tears and infectious hilarity, the capacity for burlesque or tragic evocations, the talent of complaining or of insulting.

It suffices to mention *Love of Perdition* (a great book, but not a great novel) as the apothesis of Portuguese passion, the collection of his polemical articles, and the implacable *Portrait of the Marquis de Pombal*, to see that this writer was above all a prodigy of human nature, an elemental being who found his vocation and triumph in explosions of victorious love or hate.

Oliveira Martins (1845–94) was one of those great philosopher-historians who flourished in the nineteenth century—his influence can be seen in Unamuno, Ortega y Gasset, Ramero de Maeztu and even Madariaga. He was one of the first to synthesise the common genius of the Hispano-Lusitanians in his *History of Iberian Civilization*. Other works by him are *Hellenism and Christian Civilization*, *The History of Portugal*, *The Sons of King John the First*, and *The Life of Nun Álvares* (the great hero of Portuguese history).

Now we come to the best of all Portuguese novelists, Eça de Queiroz (1843–1900), of whom Zola said: 'He is far greater than my own dear master, Flaubert.' Eça wrote *Os Maias*, *O Primo Basilio*, *A Ilustre Casa de Ramires*, *A Reliquia*, *A Cidade e as Serras*, and a volume of *Letters from England* which are as prophetic of the two last World Wars, the antagonism of the Arab World, the rise of Russia and everything else that has happened in the last sixty years as if they had been written in retrospect, not in anticipation. The above-mentioned novels are on the epic scale of Balzac, Dostoievsky, and Turgenev. *O Primo Bazilio* has a far deeper tragedy than *Madame Bovery*, because the girl involved is not a 'bitch' like Madame Bovary, but a most lovable character. Its humour and pathos alternate in an almost unbearable syncopation till the towering climax; it is one of the most tragic novels of the nineteenth century. The Portuguese accuse the early Eça of 'frenchification', but his later novels are purely Portuguese. One of the most powerful of his early novels, *The Sin of Father Amaro*, was copied by Zola in one of his anticlerical novels: but when Eça ends up, in his final works, such as *The City and the Mountains*, he turns from being the satirist of old-fashioned ideas, into the satirist of progress and progressives, with even more hilarious results. Three of these novels are already translated into English, one by Aubrey Bell, and two by myself. They are published by Reinhardt and I beg any reader who likes a good laugh (or a good cry) to read *Cousin Bazilio*, *The Relic*, or *The City and the Mountains*.

In modern criticism, the great prose history of Portuguese poetry by Gaspar Simões is the most important book for years: a monumental work.

Novelists and short story writers of today who have already made the grade in English translations are Ferreira de Castro, Miguel Torga, Dr. Fernando Namora, and Joaquim Paço d'Arcos.

CHAPTER NINE

Fado : The Music of Lisbon and the Gipsies

Fado: The Song of the Defeated. (Title of Luiz Moita's book on the *fado*.)

THERE ARE at least four forms of local popular music in modern urban civilization, which are popular in their origin as well as in their appeal. These are, in their order of fame, the *cante jondo* of the Andalusians (sometimes called flamenco music), the *fados* of the Lisbonese, the spirituals of the United States Negroes, and the calypsos of the Jamaicans. Most other 'civilized' popular music is manufactured *for* the people (not *by* the people) like the daily news, or the Light Programme.

Various derivations have been ingeniously traced for the *fado*: some have alleged its Arab origins, and others its Celtic ones. The Celtic one can easily be admitted in the receptive sense, if not as an active influence, since part-Celtic audiences are always fond of melancholy or languorous music.

'It is a degenerate successor of the *xacara* (or ballad) of the seventeenth century, as the *xacara* in its turn is a degradation of the *Romance Velho* of the fifteenth century,'[1] according to the poet, Teofilo Braga. Other authorities very naturally relate the *fado* to gipsy origins because the gipsies are, as usual, in any country where the city-underworld accepts them, the chief purveyors of entertainment, music, dance, and song, until they are enslaved, detribalized, or exterminated by modern robot states as they were in Russia, Hungary, Nazi Germany, and Republican

---

[1] Ballads comparable to our old Border ballads.

Spain. In Russia the few survivors are now being forced to work or go to gaol. Though the gipsies are the most musical people in the world, there is no distinctive gipsy music, as there is a gipsy language. None of these derivations of the *fado* need be discounted entirely, though a knockout can be given to the idea of any continuous and direct Arab influence, however remote, by pointing out that the farther south one goes in Portugal, as Moorish survivals become more and more evident in the features, costumes, and customs of the people, the latter show less and less interest in the *fado*, especially the peasants who still persist in many of the old Arab traditions, yet are either ignorant of, or completely apathetic to this form of song. Active Celtic origin is combated by Arrois on the grounds that *fado* lacks ingenuity and depends chiefly on melodrama and rhetoric.

Any Arab influences (except the faintest, most rudimentary and circuitous imaginable, *via* the gipsies, out of Andalusian music) may be discounted. The gipsies generally adapt themselves to the music of the countries where they find themselves, rather than modify the music to any racial model of their own. In Spain, quite near Lisbon, they are singing an entirely different sort of song from the *fado*. It is only in their dress and character that these otherwise chameleonic people, who would rather starve or steal than work, are conservative. Music, tauromachy, equitation, and dancing are the richer for this amiable failing of theirs. They are excellent horsemen by any standards, though their veterinary methods and horse-camouflage do not conform to our ideas. But wherever there is a horse-trade you will always hear the sound of the guitar. One of the best *fado* guitarists I know was formerly in the horse-trade; and it was he who, better than all others, performed the eel-trick on old horses (mentioned in Chapter Five) for the purpose of rendering their appearance temporarily more saleable. This is not a digression from the subject of the *fado*, since its introduction into Portugal is intimately connected with the gipsy horse-trade: and it is one of the rare examples, if not the unique one, of the gipsies having actually transferred the music of one country to another, and grafted it on to the music of the latter—instead of shedding it as they passed from the one to acquire the music of the next country. It was the crossing of the Atlantic, both ways, that prevented the gipsies from either the shedding of old, or the acquisition of new music on the way. When the Portuguese Court fled from Madrid to Brazil in 1807, during the French invasion and occupation of Lisbon under Junot, a considerable part of the population followed the Court, especially the equestrian nobles, along with all those equerries, squires, vets, farriers, saddlers, horse-breakers, attendants, grooms, postilions, and stableboys pertaining to the vast stables upon which all royal courts (even in exile) depended—not only for ceremony, travel, transport, communication and supply, but also for pleasure, amusement, exercise, hunting, and bullfighting. It was as impossible to uproot and transpose this complicated vast industry without its inveterate hangers-on, the gipsies, as it would be to uproot and transplant a big cypress tree without carrying away hundreds of barren, unproductive pebbles entangled and matted in the mud on its roots.

The gipsies were there in Brazil, in all their glory, with horses to buy and sell, just as we know them today at the fairs of Vila Franca, Golega, and Ciudad Rodrigo. We have only to look up contemporary Brazilian records to confirm it. In the excellent *Memoirs of a Sergeant of the Militia* by Manuel Antonio de Almeida,[1] written in the first half of the last century, we find this account of the transplanted gipsies in Brazil:

With the Portuguese emigrants to Brazil came also a human plague and pestilence of gipsies. A lazy people with few scruples, they soon earned and deserved the reputation of the most consummate, swindling scoundrels. Nobody who had any sense or judgment ever had any dealings with them since he was certain to be swindled out of hand. All the poetry of their customs and traditions, of which so much has been said, they left behind them on the other side of the Ocean. To Brazil they only brought with them evil habits, diabolical cunning, and villainy. They lived in complete idleness, and never passed a night except in revelry, singing, and dancing.

[1] H. Garnier, Paris 1893.

As an ex-sergeant farrier myself, and a horse-dealer in Spain and Portugal, who was only once cheated (though they tried often enough) by a gipsy during twenty years of dealing with them, I recognise in Sergeant Almeida's tone the unmistakable, authentic note of a man who has been stung by a gipsy over a horse. One can be cheated far worse, by a member of any other race, sect or nationality, and cheated of a far greater value too, without its rankling in the same way as when a gipsy stings one. It was years after he was stung that the sergeant wrote this bitter passage. When a non-gipsy cheats one, one curses the culprit and forgets, one does not curse his whole race, with his ancestors and descendants, from the beginning to the end of time, for years after, as one does with a gipsy. That was what happened to the gipsies in Brazil, where not only individual victims but the whole populace got their backs up, not with individual gipsies, but with the whole race. If a Scotsman stings me, I am angry at the time, as with a bee or a wasp as long as the pain lasts. But when a gipsy does it, it rankles afterwards, by delayed action, though one hardly even notices it at the time of being stung. It is like a mosquito bite: you only notice it, or the malaria, long after the culprit has sailed airily away, singing to himself: as when I tumbled to the fact that the most beautifully-built, seemingly flawless pannier-mule I ever bought at a bargain price was *deaf*, and therefore useless to re-sell for pannier-work to bakers, milkmen, or charcoal-sellers, since hearing is essential to their work; and their mules and donkeys should stop at the word of command in the narrow streets, always one or two doors ahead of their masters. It was a cousin of the aforementioned Lisbon gipsy *fadista* who sold me this mule in Elvas in 1935. The soreness one gets from being swindled by gipsies is not from being made a *victim*, but a *laughing-stock*. It is the spice of humour in gipsy trickery (and there was real humour in this trick played on such a gipsy-proof expert as I was till then!) that makes it rankle; and I thoroughly sympathise with the indignant militia-sergeant Almeida and his fellow-countrymen who made it so hot for the gipsies that they all had to return to Europe. It it is just possible to make a living out of *maquignonage* (or horse-trickery) where only half the population are horse-conscious, and the other half indifferent, it is much harder, in fact impossible, to do so in a country where ninety per cent of the people are horse-conscious, and moreover quicker and more serious with the knife than any gipsy could possibly be. The unpopularity of horse-trickery with such a population as then extended south of Rio to Patagonia (especially the *gauchos*) made it impossible for the gipsies to remain permanently in their new surroundings, in South America. Even British regular armies found this population far too hot and tough for them! But the time the gipsies spent in making themselves unpopular in Brazil was also spent in learning from the negroes and the workers on the ranches, plantations, and mines, a kind of song, music, and dance known as the *lundum*.

Some of the Brazilian negroes and mulattos became very adept, and after the liberation of the slaves, either came over to Portugal, or travelled around the continent of South America as wandering minstrels or *payadores*, passing round the hat, and living well on the proceeds as they rode from ranch to ranch. There is a splendid picture of one of them, together with his negro mistress, riding a-pillion on his spirited horse, in the great South American epic poem *Martin Fierro*. The competition, in Hernandez's great poem, between the Nigger and the Gaucho, Martin Fierro, in improvising verse and music, is one of the highlights of poetry in any language, and it shows to what heights some of these illiterate, anonymous, wandering poets could rise. *Martin Fierro* is a popular epic which every *gaucho* knows by heart, and unless the wandering negro musician were a recognized, by no means rare, type, Hernandez would never have introduced him into the poem (of which there is a magnificent English translation by Robert Owen).

Through the continuous poetical, choreographical, and musical exchanges between Portugal and her great young colony, certain exotic modifications began to be noticed in the Portuguese *modinha* long before the War refugees of 1807 either went to, or returned from, Brazil, though their return established the *fado* as we know it now. In the latter half of the eighteenth century the popular *modinha* came into fashion in Lisbon (in fact the word itself means the mode,[1] craze, vogue, or fashion). At first it was simply a Lisbonized version of the Italian airs sung at the big opera-houses, and remodelled by local tastes. As Senhor Luiz Moita points out in his masterly book on the *fado*, the languor of the *modinhas* was entirely foreign to the Italian arias on which they were modelled: yet it was that very languor which in the end constituted their chief characteristic. Brazilian modifications became apparent even before William Beckford, the immortal author of *Vathek*, appeared on the scene, and he was completely bowled over by the first *modinhas* he heard, opining that those who had never heard this 'original' kind of music remained in ignorance of the most enchanting melodies ever heard since the times of the Sybarites.

In a magnificent passage of his own inimitable prose, Beckford describes the languorous measures suddenly cut short as if an excess of rapture had suspended one's breathing, or as if one's soul suddenly met some 'sister' soul for which it had been longing all its life; and how these melodies insinuate themselves with careless innocence into the heart before it can steel itself against their enervating influence. He says that you imagine you are drinking milk when really the deadly, drowsy poisons of voluptuousness are penetrating into the innermost secret recesses of your being. Beckford's description of the *modinhas* would apply to many of the sweeter and softer aspects of the *fado* of today, though it has acquired more astringent ingredients. What the gipsies brought back with them from Brazil was in the nature of a fiery musical condiment to flavour the sweetness of the *modinha*: and it was this crossing of the primitive sensual ferocity and black, wailing misery of the negro *lundum* with the sweetness of the *modinha* that gave us the *fado*, with its desolating Baudelairian *miaulement*, half sensuality and half sorrow, half-delight and half-despair, and, when it takes a list towards humour, it is that macabre kind of

---

[1] *Modinha* is the diminutive of *a moda*: *la mode*.

humour we get in Villon or, even more concentratedly, in the
savagely humorous pathos of the Breton sailor-poet Tristan
Corbière.

The *lundum*, as described by early nineteenth-century travellers in Brazil, was a highly sensual song accompanied by much
belly-dancing and hip-waggling on the part of the dancers. This
sensuality disported itself against a background of black despair,
which was the popular musical expression of the negro slaves.
Negroes have rarely been anything but slaves, whether abroad, to
Europeans, Abyssinians, and Arabs: or at home to their own
tyrants: but whereas the negro slave music of North America is
more cheerful in the spirituals and plantation songs than the
African home product, the Brazilian *lunduns* are even more
gloomy. Originally, back home in Angola, and even after trans-
portation, till the mid-eighteenth century, they were nocturnal,
superstitious, divinatory, or propitiatory songs and dances, for
the purpose of driving away sickness, diverting devils, scaring
locusts, averting hailstorms, making rain, or ensuring good crops
and luck in hunting. After export to Brazil and re-exportation to
Lisbon these formerly ritual, religious, or magical incantations
emerged into the streets from the slums and brothels, having
lost their pristine innocence, but not their haunting rhythms and
hypnotic effects. Pai João (Papa John), the Brazilian counterpart
of Uncle Remus, around whom all the slave mythology, in song,
fable, anecdote, or proverb, rotates in Brazil, is a far less simple
and cheerful character than his North American confrère, though
his lot both as a slave and later a free man was much lighter (as
was that of the American Indians) under the Celtiberians than
under the race-conscious Teutons and Anglo-Saxons of North
America. But gloomy and pessimistic as Pai João may seem, the
folk art that emanated from him is more intelligent and fuses
more easily and less harmfully with European music than the
imbecile shuffle and robot cheerfulness to which the North
American negro has been degraded by despair, since Anglo-
Saxon culture offers him less outlet for development than does
the humane Portuguese civilization.

In his work *Lundum, the Grandfather of the Fado (O Lundum Avô do Fado)*, Manuel de Sousa Pinto cites the poet Filisberto Cordeiro, a romantic disciple of Bocage, who fled to Brazil in 1810 on the second French invasion of Portugal, as the first writer to mention the *fado* in print; and it was in Brazil, in connection with Brazil, that he did so. Therefore it must have first taken its shape and got its name on the other side of the Atlantic, though it acclimatized itself, found its real permanent home, and flourished so prodigiously ever since on this side. We learn also from one of its first exponents, the Brazilian mulatto poet and singer, Caldas Barbosa, that the original *fados* were accompanied (as we see from contemporary prints) only by the viola, not, as now, by both a Spanish and a Portuguese guitar of six strings. The Spanish five-stringed guitar is called the 'classical guitar' to distinguish it from the native product. When, as is generally the case, a woman sings, she holds a black shawl to her breast and leans on one of the guitarists, looking as despairing, dishevelled, ill-used, and tragic as possible.

Fado means fate, and the hardness of one's fate is the subject of all *fados*, wherein the word itself is even commoner than *amor*, *beijo*, *desejo*, and other words relating to love, kisses, and desires, which are, in nine cases out of ten, the cause of the sad fate lamented in the *fado*. *Fado*, long before it became the word used for these laments, was one of the commonest words and themes in Portuguese classical poetry. The poems of Camões swarm with allusions to his hard and bitter fate: and the next most popular Portuguese poet to Camões, Bocage, who was also, like Camões, a common sergeant in the marines, on active service in the Far East, wrote a magnificent sonnet on the very same subject of the similar *fados* or fates of himself and the sixteenth-century master. Unlike the master, Bocage was a hard case, tyrannized by his passions and vices: and the self-inflictor, as well as the victim, of his own sad fate.

The quotation of the following famous sonnet will explain better than any analysis why the word *fado* was so obviously and easily bestowed on this form of lament, for Bocage's great sonnet

N

is in mood and theme, a precursory *fado* written as a sonnet. This was scratched on the wall of Fort Jesus, the old Portuguese castle in Mombasa, probably by Bocage himself in the late eighteenth century, but it was barely legible in 1942, and was covered up with cement during the last war, when repairs were being made to the dungeons, for the old Portuguese fort is now a British prison, flying the Red Flag of the Sultan of Zanzibar; and I was able to see this sonnet when, as a sergeant with the King's African Rifles, I went to this early sixteenth-century castle to release one of my askaris, gaoled for fighting. In his book on the *fado* Senhor Moita quotes part of this sonnet as an illustration of the mood which encourages the *fado*.

> Camões! great Camões! Though twins in form,
> Tally the cursed *Fates* that love to plague us,
> Exchanging for our wineyards by the Tagus
> The sacrilegious Headland [1] and the Storm;
> Though, like yourself, from Ganges to Zambezi
> In wars and fearful penury I wander,
> On vain desires my fevered sighs to squander
> And on the thorns of memory sleep uneasy;
> Though trampled by the same vindictive doom
> I pray for sudden death to come tomorrow
> And know that peace lies only in the tomb;
> And though in shame and all precarious shifts
> You were my model—mine's the crowning sorrow
> To share your *Fate*, but not your towering gifts.

The Portuguese six-stringed guitar has developed in form since it was first married to the *fado* in the 1810s. The guitar has always been the national instrument of the Portuguese, which probably gave rise to the popular apocryphal legend about 10,000 guitars having been picked up by the Moors on the battlefield of Alcacer Kibir after the terrible disaster when King Dom Sebastian and the flower of the Portuguese nobility and army were surrounded and exterminated by the Moors in 1578. Dom Sebastian fell fighting

[1] The Cape of Good Hope, the spirit of which is personified by Camões in the *Lusiads* as the blasphemous giant, Adamastor.

in the thick of the enemy. His body was never found. There were only fifty survivors, all of whom were wounded and taken prisoners. The Portuguese have never fought better than on this occasion, though Portugal is only just recovering from it, after centuries. The King was possessed by a sublime fury. Having pursued the enemy too rashly, his troops were surrounded in small groups by overwhelming numbers, who were rallied by their own most valiant leader, Abd El-Malik. He, though on his death-bed, with a heart attack, jumped up, cursed the fleeing Arabs to turn back, and fell dead on the spot. Many ballads and laments were made about this terrible defeat and it was through them that the 'guitars of Alcacer' became a symbol, and a very apt one too, since it would not have been the first time that those lovers of misfortune, the Portuguese, have married their sombre *inamorata* in the presence of guitars.

The guitars of that epoch were of an altogether more primitive form as we see in contemporary pictures. They resembled the lutes carried by the angels in Piero della Francesca's masterpiece in the National Gallery. Zithers were also called guitars in those times, probably the two words diverged from one. Granting that they were carried into battle, as modern ones were recently by the Portuguese *Viriati* (the 30,000 Portuguese volunteers who fought in the Spanish Civil War), and granting that every *hidalgo* or knight who fought under Dom Sebastian carried one, there could not have been anything like 10,000 picked up on the field of Alcacer Kibir. In the Spanish War, both among Portuguese and Spanish, they averaged about one guitar to a platoon, and in the Spanish Legion or *Novios de la Muerte* (the *Sweethearts of Death*), where there were many Portuguese, they were generally carried by the beautiful monandrous amazons, about six to a company, who go into battle with the Legion, and always sleep with the bravest man in the bunch, till he is killed, when they swap over to the next—so much finer a system than the travelling brothels of the French Legion. Such is the death rate in the Legion that these girls are always young and beautiful, since they are always killed in action before they can age at all. They are only taken on in wartime. These modern Valkyries were treated with the greatest respect, almost worship, by the Legionaries. According to every authority who has seen it in action, from Lyautey to Rommel and Von Thoma, the Spanish Legion (for sheer combativity) is the finest fighting regiment in the world. Unlike the French Legion, only ten per cent of it is composed of foreigners, mostly Portuguese, and there were several Portuguese platoons, and a White Russian one, also with a guitar.

On the night before the Spanish army's crossing of the Sigre, the most impressive thing I ever saw in my life, when the whole army knelt at Mass before dawn in those icy highlands, and then plunged chest-deep into the ice-cold water to victory, it was uncanny to hear before lights-out the sultry sound of a *fado*, which I had never imagined could be sung outside of a crowded café in a smoke-filled atmosphere, but even there, transposed so far out of its element amongst the snow-peaks, it seemed to gain rather than lose that weird piercing and hypnotic magic that it has in a crowd, in a smoky, wine-fuming *boite-de-nuit*, which is its true atmosphere. When next day I stumbled over several armless, discarded torsos of guitars plugged with bullet-holes, they seemed almost as human and pathetic as the dead around them, who had also lost their voices so suddenly after all the cheering, singing, and shouting of the advance. Guitars have, owing to their lovely female curves, always been popular subjects for still-lives. Even to this day, in Lisbon, when I am in the crowded Luso, Mesquita, Tipoia, or Faia, or other *fado* 'joints', with British friends who wish to hear the *fado*, I never see a Portuguese guitar without recalling that strangest and stillest of 'still-lives' composed by dead guitars and men in the icy haunts of the eagle, the bear, and the wolf, on the slopes of the Pyrenees, so utterly and oppositely different from the scene of their origin.

In the singing of the *fado*, the player of the Portuguese guitar plays every note of the actual tune of the song, and the other player strums the accompaniment on the Spanish guitar. For a long time what is now known as the 'Portuguese guitar' was known as the 'English guitar'. As it increased in popularity the importation of this commodity, in great numbers, from England, became an integral factor of exchange in the port wine trade in the early nineteenth century. But then an Englishman named Simpson began to manufacture the instrument in Portugal, and it gradually became a native product. A highly sophisticated side-line, or offshoot, of the *fado* is to be found amongst the students of the ancient university of Coimbra: but apart from that the *fado* is exclusively Lisbonese and as metropolitan as a Cockney accent. It is not the national music. There is no Porto school of *fado*, as there is a definite Porto school of poetry.

Modern bullfighting is of the same age, and developed along the same lines, as the *fado*. You will always find them hand in hand in Lisbon. The wall-paintings in the *fado* cafés and restaurants are generally of bullfights. Both modern bullfighting and *fado* are the results of the proletarianising of the arts of tauromachy and music: they both owe a great deal indirectly to the French Revolution, and their formation is contemporary with, and a result of the impoverishment by the wars, the upheavals and long exile of many Portuguese, which emanated from the doubtful benefit. Music and musical instruments had been chiefly in the hands of the rich, and it was they who patronised, fed and clothed the composers. Bullfighting had been practised as an equestrian sport, like jousting amongst the knights and gentlemen. The greatest toreadors in the golden age of Spain and Portugal were highborn nobles like Cæsar Borgia, the poet Conde de Villamediana, Saint Francisco Borgia (while he was still a duke) and King Dom Sebastian: similarly the Portuguese composers and performers of the imitation Italian opera then in fashion, were wooed and protected by the Court, the Cardinal, and the wealthy nobility.

Pedestrian working-class *toreros* only became popular about the same time that music left the opera and went to the slums and the stews, and the uproarious, picturesque bohemian life that was typified in, and dominated by the romantically diabolical figure of Bocage, before his exile, repentance, and untimely death. Byron is generally thought of as the first of these wild,

reckless romantics, but Bocage preceded him by many years, and
was the first of that Don Juanesque type we find in Byron, Pushkin, Liszt, Musset, Lermontov, Espronceda, and later in Lautré-
amont, Rimbaud, Darío, and Chocano. Beckford writes of
Bocage, whom he calls by his Christian name Manuel Maria, as
perhaps 'the most original poet ever created by God', and gives
an unforgettable picture of this dionysiac character and the
hypnotic power by which he could at one moment enrapture and
at another moment petrify his hearers. In this weird night life of
Lisbon, bullfighters, fado-singers, nobles, pimps and prostitutes
all jostled together. The famous *fado* singer Maria Severa became
a legend for her amours and the knifings, jealousies, and battles
which went on around her. She had an affair with the great
Mæcenas and champion *rejoneador* of Portuguese bullfighting,
the most popular man at that time; and with the finest horseman
in Portugal, the Count of Vimioso, who is still remembered in
many a popular *fado* and street-song, partly for the sumptuous
bullfighting displays he gave for the people at his palace in the
Campo Grande, then just outside Lisbon; but chiefly because of
his affair with Maria Severa.

Just after the time of Vimioso many noblemen began to fight
on foot, and wrestle bulls as *forcados*, such as the famous Calleya
Cruz who also enjoyed the favours of many illustrious dames of
the nobility besides those of famous *fadistas*, who were by then
getting more 'respectable', thus carrying on the tradition which
seems to have wedded the *fado* to the bullfight inseparably since
the days of Maria Severa. The black shawl worn by *fadistas* is
said to be in mourning for Maria, who, amongst other queer facts
of her life, was the daughter of a bearded woman tavern-keeper,
and who died at the age of twenty-six from over-eating roasted
pigeons. She is an almost Rabelaisian character, and much of the
legend that has grown up around her is apocryphal. But it is very
likely that Maria Severa always wore a black shawl herself as most
women do in Portugal, not for mourning, but use.

The Conde de Vimioso's somewhat morbid taste for the most
plebeian types of singers (most of whom in those days combined

prostitution with music) was shared also by his precursors, the bullfighting Conde de Prado and a nephew of the Conde de Lippe, which gave rise to a rollicking anonymous ballad reminiscent of Burns' *Jolly Beggars*, or Skelton's *Eleanor Running*, called the *Dance with the Sluts*. This indicates that it was the exception rather than the rule for the aristocracy to make fools of themselves in this way, since the satirist fairly holds his sides with laughter and makes us do so too: but the text is too coarse for publication and we are a long way in this lively satire from the sympathetic, sentimentalised anti-snob pornography of *Lady Chatterley*.

When the Court finally returned from Brazil to Lisbon in 1824, preceded by half, and followed by half the gipsy emigrants, the *fado*–bullfighting alliance was given an enormous lift, both from above and from the lower levels, attaining a measure of respectability and greater popularity, for amongst the returned exiles was the redoubtable, fiery Prince Charming, singer of *fados*, dancer of *fandangos*, breaker of horses, and fighter of bulls (a cross between Prince Hal and Bonny Prince Charlie, both of whose bloods coursed in his veins), the picador-Infante, Dom Miguel, aged nineteen, who was not slow to place himself on the throne, dissolve the parliament, restore for the time being the old traditionalist idea of monarchy, delight the majority of his subjects, and scandalize the rest, especially the General Staff, by reviewing his cavalry in the costume of a *campino* of the Ribatejo, and his infantry in that of a *forcado*, or foot-torero. He was a real king, and, as such, adored by the poorest and humblest of his subjects, who had seen Junot, Massina, and other invaders welcomed by delegations of freemasons and liberals, and, on one or two occasions, when the lower orders had got out of hand, had mobbed and torn the traitors.

According to Wellington's correspondence, it was the liberals and masons who acted as the fifth column for the invading French forces throughout the peninsula, delivering up forts and towns without resistance to their French confrères of the Grand Orient. The same has happened in two or three subsequent wars. Peninsular politics until recently were a see-saw between the national, patriotic, clerical-cum-royalist forces on the extreme right, and anticlerical-cum-masonic forces on the extreme left. According to the fortunes of the nationalists, the fortunes of the *fadistas* and bullfighters rose and fell. In Spain, Godoy, the queen lover, a liberal freemason, and the virtual dictator, even went so far as to abolish bullfighting and flamenco-singing: and it was a serious setback to Portuguese music and tauromachy when Dom Miguel was deposed, and replaced by his brother, Dom Pedro, a liberal mason, against the national will, with the aid of a large army of French and English troops. Dom Miguel is still mourned by the peasants and the poor. Under Dom Pedro there was endless frenchification and republicanization, religious orders were expelled, and Brazil, revolting, was lost to the great Portuguese empire, and Dom Miguel, the friend of the *fado*, ended his days in Vienna: but in spite of all reforms and setbacks, the *fado* has survived to this day.

From the dark period of the bitter Miguelite Civil Wars that raged between 1828 and 1847, there has remained little written evidence as to the development and evolution of the *fado*, but it emerged with two guitars and a much wider repertoire, having been promoted from the slums and the stews into the more respectable bourgeois quarters. It was no longer apache-music from 1848 onwards. Its enemies (and they were many—especially the Church) regarded it as a harmful drug, a national menace, a habit-forming narcotic, to which the people clung fatalistically and suicidally, while it allegedly rotted the will and the mind of the nation. Forty years ago, when the decadence of Portugal reached its depths, such an argument could have been propounded with every appearance of reason, but today, and for the last thirty years, the hold of the *fado* has not diminished in the second rebirth and prosperity of Portugal. In the new Lisbon the *fado* still flourished, in a city which is in every way the antithesis of the Lisbon of dead cats, rubbish-heaps, and mouldering palaces, described by Beckford and Fielding. It has become a city of air, light, cleanliness, hanging gardens, flowering avenues, and open thoroughfares. Yet, even here, the melancholy, 'morbid' *fado* has more or less proved not only its permanence but its complete innocuousness as regards the morale of the nation, and its absolute necessity to some strange atavistic hunger in the hearts of the Lisbonese, who, despite the melancholy of their songs, are full of gaiety and fun.

The great Portuguese poet, Fernando Pessoa, who died in 1935, explains the *fado* in this way: 'All poetry (and what is song but aided poetry?) reflects the spirit which it does not contain. That is why the songs of sad nations are gay, and those of gay nations are sad.' This would seem to agree with Yeats' dictum that poets, in their writing, are the opposite of what they are in real life: for instance, the irrepressible, loquacious, violent, fidgety, and vociferous Landor wrote concise little poems of Olympian calm; 'kind Kit Marlowe' revelled in blood, thunder, and cruelty; and so on. But this is far from being a rule: most of the few poets I have known personally are exactly like their work—Edith Sitwell, Paul Valéry, T. S. Eliot, Dylan Thomas, William Empson; I could never have imagined them different from what they are. But racially speaking there is a lot in what Pessoa said. It is the Scandinavians and Germans who have the gayest songs, who commit the most suicides. Anyway, so far, the government has never had to ban or censor *fados* at any time in Portugal, as the Hungarians had to forbid the song *Sombre Sunday* on account of the number of suicides that followed each broadcast. There were even discussions in the French press as to whether the French version *Sombre Dimanche* should be allowed, when it became a craze in Montmartre. But I cannot trace any similar epidemic of suicides in Paris.

From the well-fed appearance of most singers and accompanists of these plaintive, seedy, but often extremely beautiful songs, one gets the idea that suicide from anything but over-eating, as in Maria Severa's case, would be almost an impossibility. Perhaps it would be as well to end up this account of the fado by quoting a verse to illustrate the philosophic attitude of at least one Lisbonese *fadista* to the misfortune which is the theme of all his songs.

> I bask and revel in my woes
> That with my mood so well agree
> I feel compassionate for those
> Who feel compassionate for me.

The war against the *fado* is still being waged by the more virile spirits of the younger generation, but without shaking its hold on the metropolis and without making the slightest impression on the 'healthier' songs of Alentejo or of the muscular north of Portugal, where self-organized groups called *Ranchos* keep up the old songs and dances without any of the arts-and-craftsy, self-conscious supervision, patronage and spurious jollity given to morris dancing and other revivals of folk-lore in England. For there is no revival in this case: the *ranchos* have always existed just as they are.

It is in the month of October, during the most ancient of all Portuguese festivals, that of the grape-harvest, that you hear the best singing in places like Amarante and Lamego, song that is full of 'sunburnt mirth', love of life, and vibrant stimulating melody: but no one passing through Lisbon should miss spending one night with the *fadistas*.

CHAPTER TEN
A Word About Lisbon

JUST A FINAL word about that wonderful city, Lisbon, of which the new modern part equals in beauty the ancient part that survived the earthquake.

In the old days, when the Spanish and Portuguese loved each other, as they are learning to do again, Tirso de Molina wrote about Lisbon—a poet as great as our Shakespeare, the creator of types equally gigantic or monstrous, the originator of *Don Juan*, *Tartuffe*, *L'Amour Medecin*, and almost everything that arch-plagiarist Molière could prosify, sissify, and emasculate into cripples' crutches from these majestic Toledan oaks, whittling them into sticks!

Lope, Camões, Calderon, Gil Vicente, Cervantes (especially in *Numancia*), Ruiz de Alarcon, and the rest of the Iberian galaxy of the golden age, equal (if they do not excel) our British Elizabethans. The British hatred of 'dagoes' due to the thundering defeats, routs, and surrenders at the Antilles and Buenos Aires and Oriamendi, of Raleigh, Drake, Hawkins, Cobham, Brooke, Beresford, Lacy Evans, etc. (if it did not date from the resounding thump that the Black Prince took back with him to die of chagrin and fright at Bordeaux) has resulted in a voluntary misunderstanding and underrating, in England, of this superb literature, only paralleled by the Hebrews, the Greeks, and the English themselves—those perishers!—who infatuate and exasperate me equally (wonderful soldiers—utterly ignorant diplomats, and destroyers of the Universe!).

This is what Tirso wrote of Lisbon, which has now been restored to its original greatness by the Grace of Our Lady of Fatima and by the judicious prudence, dauntless courage, honesty, and determination of her great, 'illuminated' and faithful servant, Oliveira Salazar. In all my books I have to end up singing, so here it is. This (in English), my dear reader, is what the great poet and Lusophile, Tirso, wrote about Lisbon. It cost me a lot of midnight oil and sweat to translate it—but it's been thrice on the Third Programme and praised in *The Times*. Some of the features of the landscape disappeared in the earthquake, but it's a pretty fair idea of Lisbon from the Rossio to the harbour.

As a matter of fact, being almost a native of the Tagus, and having hymned Toledo, the incomparable Minerva [1] of all cities, the anti-Koestlerite, anti-Hemingway, and anti-Spenderite acropolis of the West (where we flogged the Reds), I shall try most faithfully, gratefully, and lovingly to translate this great master's Hymn of Praise to Lisbon. With this poem from the Commander's speech in the *Burlador de Sevilla* [2] (the *Trickster of Seville*) which had such a success on the B.B.C., I take leave of my readers hoping I have given them a laugh or two (because that is partly what life seems to have been invented for!). But also there is plenty of room for thanks, wonder and admiration. And here is Tirso's grateful, wondering, and admiring description of Lisbon, which, even in translation, seems to 'come across'. It is not only a perfect description physically, but the finest description of Lisbon's Christian imperial mission as it was then, and is again now, as restored and revived by the miracle of Fatima and the genius of Salazar.

> I'll paint a picture of it in the air.
>
> I'd like to hear it—someone fetch a chair.
>
> Why, Lisbon is the world's eighth wonder.

---

[1] I should rather say the Shulamite of all cities for the Hebrews made it in 1000 years B.C. and most of the heroic inhabitants take after the type, pertinacious, poetical and heroic.

[2] The *Burlador of Sevilla* is the original and greatest of all the Don Juans, was the original much demeaned by Molière and then taken up by Mozart, Byron, Pushkin and others.

Out of the inmost heart of Spain,
Which lies about the hills of Cuenca,
The Tagus rolls a sumptuous train,
And, having traversed half that country,
Then enters the Atlantic main,
Along the sacred banks of Lisbon's
Proud city on the southern side.
But just before its course and name
Get lost forever in the tide,
It forms a port on the Sierras,
Where ships of all the navies ride
That can be numbered in this world.
Like mustered pines in black battalions
The masts of dhows, feluccas, schooners
Of Turks, of Norsemen or Italians,
Of carracks, caravels and sloops,
Of barques and galleys, junks and galleons
Are crowded in such countless troops
They form a vast and flowering city
Where Neptune reigns, for miles inland!
Towards that part where sets the Sun,
Guarding the port, on either hand
Of where the Tagus makes an entry,
(One called Cascais and one Saint John)
Two mighty fortresses keep sentry
With many a grimly snouted gun
Earth's mightiest strongholds each well able
The navies of the world to stun.
Just half a league from town there stands
Belem, the convent of Jerome,
Who for his guardian had a lion
And for his talisman a stone,
Whom Catholic and Christian princes
Are keeping their eternal home.
Passing the vast and splendid fabric
Beyond Alcantara, you sally

A league, to reach Jaregas Convent
Which fills a wide and lovely valley,
That is encircled by three slopes
Here, with his paintbrush, would Apelles
Have to renounce his proudest hopes:
For seen far off, it seems as if
Clusters of pearls hang from the skies
Within whose clear immensity
Ten Romes appear to multiply
In labyrinths of convents, churches
And towers, with highways streaming by,
With many a vast estate and mansion
Extending to the sea and,
And all in infinite expansion,
Through Empires, sowing deathless seeds
Wherever thoughts of man can fly,
In building, missions, arts, in deeds
Of valour, verse that cannot die,
And flawless rectitude of laws
But reaching nearest to the sky
Of all the glories that I saw
The summit of her Christian pity
And most of all to be adored
The peak of the Imperial city
Her Hospital—Misericorde.
The thing most worthy of amaze
That in this wondrous pile I found
Was that from its high top the gaze
For seven leagues can sweep its rays
On sixty villages all round.
And all of them the sea through bays
Could reach, and at their doors was found.

Date Due

	PRINTED	IN U. S. A.	